Lab Manu

Environmental Science

PEARSON

AGS Globe

Shoreview, Minnesota

Pearson AGS Globe™ is a trademark of Pearson Education, Inc.
Pearson® is a registered trademark of Pearson plc.

ISBN 0-7854-3952-8

A 0 9 8 7 6 5 4 3 2 1

1-800-328-2560
www.agsglobe.com

Table of Contents

Table of Contents, continued

Table of Contents, continued

Environmental Science

Safety Rules and Symbols

In this book, you will learn about environmental science through investigations and labs. During these activities, it is important to follow safety rules, procedures, and your teacher's directions. You can avoid accidents by following directions and handling materials carefully. Read and follow the safety rules below, and learn the safety symbols. To alert you to possible dangers, safety symbols will appear with each investigation or lab. Reread the rules below often and review what the symbols mean.

General Safety

◆ Read each Express Lab, Investigation, and Discovery Investigation before doing it. Review the materials list and follow the safety symbols and safety alerts.

◆ Ask questions if you do not understand something.

◆ Never perform an experiment, mix substances, or use equipment without permission.

◆ Keep your work area clean and free of clutter.

◆ Be aware of other students working near you.

◆ Do not play or run during a lab activity. Take your lab work seriously.

◆ Know where fire extinguishers, fire alarms, first aid kits, fire blankets, and the nearest telephone are located. Be familiar with the emergency exits and evacuation route from your room.

◆ Keep your hands away from your face.

◆ Immediately report all accidents to your teacher, including injuries, broken equipment, and spills.

Flame/Heat Safety

◆ Clear your work space of materials that could burn or melt.

◆ Before using a burner, know how to operate the burner and gas outlet.

◆ Be aware of all open flames. Never reach across a flame.

◆ Never leave a flame or operating hot plate unattended.

◆ Do not heat a liquid in a closed container.

◆ When heating a substance in a test tube or flask, point the container away from yourself and others.

◆ Do not touch hot glassware or the surface of an operating hot plate or lightbulb.

◆ In the event of a fire, tell your teacher and leave the room immediately.

◆ If your clothes catch on fire, stop, drop to the floor, and roll.

Safety Rules and Symbols, continued

Electrical Safety

♦ Never use electrical equipment near water, on wet surfaces, or with wet hands or clothing.

♦ Alert your teacher to any frayed or damaged cords or plugs.

♦ Before plugging in equipment, be sure the power control is in the "off" position.

♦ Do not place electrical cords in walkways or let cords hang over table edges.

♦ Electricity flowing in wire causes the wire to become hot. Use caution.

♦ Turn off and unplug electrical equipment when you are finished using it.

Chemical Safety

♦ Check labels on containers to be sure you are using the right substance.

♦ Do not directly smell any substance. If you are instructed to smell a substance, gently fan your hand over the substance, waving its vapors toward you.

♦ When handling substances that give off gases or vapors, work in a fume hood or well-ventilated area.

♦ Do not taste any substance. Never eat, drink, or chew gum in your work area.

♦ Do not return unused chemicals to their original containers.

♦ Avoid skin contact with chemicals. Some chemicals can irritate or harm skin.

♦ If a chemical spills on your clothing or skin, rinse the area immediately with plenty of water. Tell your teacher.

♦ When diluting an acid or base with water, always add the acid or base to the water. Do not add water to the acid or base.

♦ Wash your hands after working with chemicals.

Eye Protection

♦ Wear safety goggles at all times or as directed by your teacher.

♦ If a chemical gets in your eyes or on your face, use an eyewash station or flush your eyes and face with running water immediately. Tell your teacher.

Animal Safety

♦ Do not touch or approach an animal without your teacher's permission.

♦ Handle and care for animals only as your teacher directs.

♦ If you are bitten, stung, or scratched by an animal, tell your teacher.

♦ Do not expose animals to loud noises, overcrowding, or other stresses.

♦ Wash your hands after touching an animal.

Safety Rules and Symbols, continued

Hand Safety

◆ Wear protective gloves when working with chemicals or solutions. Wear gloves for handling preserved specimens and plants.

◆ Do not touch an object that could be hot.

◆ Use tongs or utensils to hold a container over a heat source.

◆ Wash your hands when you are finished with a lab activity.

Plant Safety

◆ Do not place any part of a plant in your mouth. Do not rub plant parts or liquids on your skin.

◆ Wear gloves when handling plants or as directed by your teacher.

◆ Wash your hands after handling any part of a plant.

Glassware Safety

◆ Check glassware for cracks or chips before use. Give broken glassware to your teacher; do not use it.

◆ Keep glassware away from the edge of a work surface.

◆ If glassware breaks, tell your teacher. Dispose of glass according to your teacher's directions.

Clothing Protection

◆ Wear a lab coat or apron at all times or as directed by your teacher.

◆ Tie back long hair, remove dangling jewelry, and secure loose-fitting clothing.

◆ Do not wear open-toed shoes, sandals, or canvas shoes in the lab.

Sharp Object Safety

◆ Take care when using scissors, pins, scalpels, or pointed tools or blades.

◆ Cut objects on a suitable work surface. Cut away from yourself and others.

◆ If you cut yourself, notify your teacher.

Cleanup/Waste Disposal

◆ If a chemical spills, alert your teacher and ask for clean up instructions.

◆ Follow your teacher's directions to dispose and clean up substances.

◆ Turn off burners, water faucets, electrical equipment, and gas outlets.

◆ Clean equipment if needed and return it to its proper location.

◆ Clean your work area and work surface.

◆ Wash your hands when you are finished.

Express Lab 1

Use with Express Lab 1, page 6

Materials   paper

          pencil

Procedure

1. Look around your classroom. Observe and write down the things that surround you.

2. Identify which natural resources might have been used to make these things.

3. List all the natural resources you identified.

Analysis

1. Which natural resources are used to construct buildings?

   _____

   _____

2. Which natural resources on your list will be used up or eaten? One example is an apple someone brought for lunch.

   _____

   _____

3. Which natural resources do you share with other students? One example is the water in the drinking fountain.

   _____

   _____

Plants, Nature's Energy Converters

Plants are very important to the environment. Plants change the sun's energy into a food energy that animals can use. The food that plants make is a sugar called glucose. Extra glucose is stored in plants as starch.

In this lab, you will use iodine to test a leaf for starch. Iodine is a chemical that turns black in the presence of starch.

Materials

safety goggles	tap water	iodine solution (weak solution of iodine and water or Lugol's solution)
lab coat or apron	isopropyl alcohol	
hot plate	geranium leaf	
600-mL beaker	petri dish	rectangle of black paper, 2 cm x 1 cm
250-mL beaker	forceps	
beaker tongs	small paper clip	

Procedure, Day 1

1. Fold the rectangle of black paper in half. Use a paper clip to place the paper around a section of a geranium leaf on a plant. The folded paper should cover the top and bottom of the leaf.

2. Place the plant in a sunny place for three days.

Procedure, Day 4

1. Put on safety goggles and a lab coat or apron.

2. After three days, take the leaf off of the plant and remove the black paper.

3. Add 300 mL of water to the 600-mL beaker. Place the beaker on the hot plate.

4. Turn on the hot plate and bring the water to a slow, rolling boil.

5. Pinch the stem from the leaf. Use forceps to place the leaf into the boiling water. Let the leaf boil for about one minute.

6. Pour 100 mL of alcohol into the 250-mL beaker.

7. Remove the leaf from the water and place it in the alcohol.

8. Hold the beaker with tongs. Slowly lower the beaker of alcohol into the boiling water beaker.

Plants, Nature's Energy Converters, continued

9. Keep the beaker in the boiling water until the alcohol turns dark green.

10. Turn off the hot plate and remove the leaf from the alcohol. Place it flat in the petri dish, top-side down.

11. Add two or three drops of iodine to the leaf. Watch for the leaf to turn black. This may take a few minutes.

Cleanup/Disposal

Follow your teacher's instructions for cleanup and disposal.

Analysis

1. Why do you think the alcohol turned green when the leaf was boiled?

   _____

2. Why do you think the green pigment had to be removed from the leaf?

   _____

3. Could you tell where the black paper had been on the leaf before you added the iodine?

   _____

Conclusions

1. In what areas did the leaf turn black? _____

2. In what part of the leaf was starch made? _____

3. What does a plant need in order to make starch? _____

   _____

Explore Further

Repeat this experiment with a plant placed in a dark room for three days. Record the results.

_____

_____

_____

Understanding Earth's History

Use with Investigation 1, pages 17–18

Earth was created approximately 4.6 billion years ago. However, life did not appear until over one billion years later. Even after the first basic signs of life, it took over three billion more years for the first pre-humans to appear. This lab will help you visualize period of time during Earth's long history.

Timeline	
4.6 billion years ago	Earth and planets formed
3.7 billion years ago	Earth's crust hardened
3.5 billion years ago	first life in the oceans; photosynthesis begins
650 million years ago	first multicellular organisms appear
500 million years ago	first land plants
250 million years ago	mass extinction (99 percent of life disappears)
245 million years ago	age of reptiles begins
200 million years ago	continents drift apart
65 million years ago	age of dinosaurs ends with mass extinction (70 percent of life disappears)
3.5 million years ago	first prehumans appear
100,000 years ago	first *Homo sapiens* appear
10,000 years ago	first record of human history
4,500 years ago	pyramids were built
650 years ago	Black Death
270 years ago	beginning of the Industrial Revolution
230 years ago	birth of the United States

Materials   460 pennies   timeline   4 index cards   marker

Understanding Earth's History, continued

Procedure

1. Place the pennies in one large pile. These pennies represent Earth's history.

2. Mark the index cards A, B, C, and D.

3. Divide the pennies into two piles. Put 110 pennies in Pile A and 350 pennies in Pile B. Pile A represents the time period from the appearance of life to the present time.

4. Take 65 pennies from Pile B and place them in Pile C. This third pile shows how long organisms with more than one cell have existed.

5. Take one penny from Pile C and place it in Pile D. This represents the last 10 million years of Earth's history. The time period since *Homo sapiens* appeared would be one-hundredth of this penny.

Cleanup/Disposal

Return the pennies to your teacher. Wash your hands with soap and warm water.

Analysis

1. How would you represent recorded human history using these pennies?

   _____

   _____

2. How would you represent the point when dinosaurs became extinct?

   _____

   _____

Conclusions

1. How many years does each penny represent?

   _____

   _____

2. What type of life has been present through most of Earth's history?

   _____

   _____

Explore Further

Create your own timeline by using a meter stick and a piece of tape.
Measure out the amount of time for each event from left to right.

Mud Puddles as Mini-Ecosystems

Ecosystems are all around you. Not all ecosystems are large, however. They can be as small as a mud puddle or the water in a roadside ditch. Small ecosystems like these are often referred to as mini-ecosystems. Organisms in these and other ecosystems interact with each other and the environment.

In this lab, you will look for evidence of organisms within a mini-ecosystem.

Materials   safety goggles
            lab coat or apron
            hand shovel
            white poster board
            magnifying glass
            2 large cups
            disposable gloves

Procedure

1. Go outdoors and find a mud puddle or a ditch of standing water. Put on safety goggles, a lab coat or apron, and the disposable gloves.

2. Use one cup to scoop up some of the water in the puddle.

3. Use the hand shovel to dig up some mud from the puddle. Place this mud in the other cup.

4. When you return to the lab, spread the mud you collected onto a piece of poster board. Make it about 2 centimeters thick.

5. Look in the mud for living things or evidence of living things. Evidence could include parts of dead plants or animals. In your notebook, write down what you see.

6. Use the magnifying glass to examine the cup of water. Look for living things or evidence of living things. In your notebook, write down what you see.

Cleanup/Disposal

Follow your teacher's instructions for cleanup and disposal.

Mud Puddles as Mini-Ecosystems, continued

Analysis

1. What evidence of animal life did you see?

_____

_____

2. What evidence of plant life did you see?

_____

_____

3. Describe any organisms you could only see by using a magnifying glass.

_____

_____

Conclusions

1. What makes a mud puddle a mini-ecosystem?

_____

_____

2. Which organisms in the mud puddle do you think have the highest numbers? Explain your answer.

_____

_____

Explore Further

Repeat this experiment with mud and water from a pond. Compare how they are similar to the samples from the mud puddle.

_____

_____

_____

_____

Using the Scientific Method
Use with Discovery Investigation 1, pages 30–31

Scientists answer questions and solve problems in an orderly way. They use
a series of steps called the scientific method. How can you use the scientific
method to answer questions? You will find out in this lab.

Plants need several things to grow well. Among them are light, space, and air.
Also, plants need liquids, but the amount and type of liquid used can vary. How
important are these variables for plant growth?

Materials   safety goggles

lab coat or apron

2 plastic cups

20 bean seeds

potting soil

water

vinegar

lamp

paper towels

eyedropper

Procedure

1. In a small group, discuss the question in the second paragraph above.
   Then write a hypothesis that you can test with an experiment. Choose one
   variable to test: amount of light or water, or the type of liquid used.

2. Write a procedure for your experiment, including any Safety Alerts.
   Use materials from the Materials list. The experiment should take eight
   days to complete.

3. Be sure your experiment changes, or tests, only one variable at a time.
   Include a control group in which you do not change any variables.

4. Draw a data table to record your data for eight days.

5. Have your entire procedure approved by your teacher. Then carry out
   your experiment.

Using the Scientific Method, continued

Cleanup/Disposal

Before leaving the lab, clean up your materials and wash your hands.

Analysis

1. What variable did you change in this experiment?

   _____

   _____

2. What changes did you see among the bean seeds after Day 4? What changes did you see after Day 8?

   _____

   _____

Conclusions

1. Was your hypothesis supported by the results of your investigation? Explain.

   _____

   _____

2. What problems did you have in performing the experiment? What part of the procedure would you change to be more successful?

   _____

   _____

Explore Further

In your group, discuss the variables of plant growth that you did not test. Pick one of these variables to investigate in the future. Write a procedure to carry out your investigation.

_____

_____

_____

_____

Express Lab 2

Use with Express Lab 2, page 47

Materials   safety goggles

lab coat or apron

cereal bowl

small plastic or paper cup

vinegar

red food coloring

spoon

baking powder

Procedure

1. Put on safety goggles and a lab coat or apron.

2. Place the bowl upside down in the pie pan.

3. Fill the cup two-thirds full with vinegar. Add the food coloring and stir.

4. Set the cup on top of the bowl, and add a spoonful of baking powder.

Analysis

1. What caused the "lava" to flow out of the "volcano"?

_____

_____

2. What happened to the gases in the "lava" bubbles?

_____

_____

The Carbon Dioxide-Oxygen Cycle

Plants and animals are dependant upon each other for survival. Plants take up the carbon dioxide that animals exhale. They use the carbon dioxide to make sugar. During this process, plants give off oxygen gas. Animals inhale the oxygen and use it to make energy.

In this lab, you will work with bromthymol blue (BTB), an indicator. Carbon dioxide causes BTB to change from blue to yellow or green. You will uses BTB to show that animals produce carbon dioxide.

Materials
safety goggles	pond snail (medium-sized)
lab coat or apron	100-mL beaker
BTB solution	plastic wrap
dropper	75 mL water

Procedure

1. Draw a data table like the one below on a sheet of paper.

2. Put on safety goggles and a lab coat or apron.

3. Add 75 mL of water to a 100-mL beaker.

4. Add drops of BTB solution to the beaker until the water turns blue.

5. Record the color of the water in your data table.

6. Place a snail in the beaker of BTB solution and water. Cover the beaker with plastic wrap.

7. Place the beaker in a well-lit area for 24 hours. Do not place the beaker in direct sun.

8. After 24 hours, observe the beaker. Record any color change in your data table.

Data Table

Color in beaker before snail	Color in beaker after snail

The Carbon Dioxide-Oxygen Cycle, continued

Cleanup/Disposal
Follow your teacher's directions for cleanup and disposal.

Analysis

1. What color was the water in the beaker before you added the snail?

_____

2. What color was the water after you added the snail?

_____

3. Why do you think the color of the water changed?

_____

Conclusions

1. Why did you use BTB in this experiment?

_____

_____

2. What gas is produced by snails? How do you know?

_____

_____

Explore Further

What would happen if you put a piece of water plant in a beaker of BTB?
Write your prediction on your paper.

_____

_____

_____

_____

Cloud Formation

Use with Investigation 2, pages 60–61

Cloud formation is part of the water cycle. A cloud forms when water in the air condenses. The air always contains some water, but clouds are not always present. Why? In this lab, you will use a model to make a cloud. You will then observe the conditions that cause cloud formation.

Materials   safety goggles

lab coat or apron

2-liter clear plastic bottle with cap

water

temperature strip

matches

Procedure

1. Put on safety goggles and a lab coat or apron.

2. Place a small amount of water and a temperature strip in the plastic bottle.

3. Strike a match, blow it out, and drop the match in the mouth of the bottle. **Safety Alert: Be careful when working with fire.**

4. To capture some of the smoke, put the cap on the bottle quickly and tighten it.

5. Squeeze the bottle and then release it.

6. Observe what happens and record what you see.

Cleanup/Disposal

Follow your teacher's instructions to clean up and dispose of your materials.

Cloud Formation, continued

Analysis

1. What do you see inside the bottle when you squeeze it?

_____

2. What do you see inside the bottle when you release it?

_____

3. What does the smoke add to the bottle?

_____

4. What happens to the temperature strip when you squeeze the bottle?

_____

Conclusions

1. Under what conditions do clouds form?

_____

_____

2. What process is happening as the cloud forms?

_____

_____

Explore Further

Repeat the procedure with no smoke in the bottle. Try the procedure using a dry bottle with no water or smoke. Sit or stand on the capped bottle to apply more pressure. Observe how the temperature changes as you increase and decrease the pressure in the bottle.

_____

_____

_____

_____

The Big Breakup

The earth's crust is made of moveable plates. At one time, the plates of continents were joined together. They formed a single landmass called Pangaea. As the earth cooled, Pangaea began to crack and break apart.

In this lab, you will construct a model of the breakup of Pangaea.

Materials   colored pencils or crayons: red, orange, yellow, green, blue, purple, tan
scissors
copy of a map of Pangaea (from the Internet)
copy of a map of the world (from the Internet)

Procedure

1. Look at a current map of the world. Compare it to the map of Pangaea. Use the map to help you identify landmasses on Pangaea that look like today's continents. On both maps, color the landmasses according to the following table.

Landmasses	Color
North and South America	Yellow
Australia	Tan
India	Orange
Africa	Green
Europe and Asia	Red
Antarctica	Blue
Greenland	Purple

2. Use scissors to cut out the landmasses on the map of Pangaea.
Safety Alert: Handle the scissors carefully.

3. Place each colored landmass of Pangaea on top of the continent it resembles.

The Big Breakup, continued

Analysis

1. How many continents exist today?

_____

2. How many continents existed at the time of Pangaea?

_____

Conclusions

1. Over millions of years, what happened to the landmasses of Pangaea?

_____

_____

2. How did the changes in Pangaea affect the sizes of the oceans?

_____

_____

3. When two plates collide, land can be pushed to form mountain ranges. Using a world map, identify two locations where mountain ranges exist.

_____

_____

Explore Further

Predict the position of the earth's continents in the distant future. Make a drawing of the continents from your prediction.

Mountain Building

Use with Discovery Investigation 2, pages 73–74

Mountain building is a very slow process. However, the results are dramatic. In this lab, you will model one way that mountains form. Then you will develop a procedure for showing how mountains change over time.

Materials	safety goggles
	lab coat or apron
	clear plastic box
	particle board
	dry sand
	metric ruler
	flour
	scoop

Procedure

1. Put on safety goggles and a lab coat or apron.

2. Work with a partner. Place the particle board at one end of the box.

3. Pour enough sand in the box to make a layer about 2 cm thick. Use a ruler to level off the sand.

4. Spread a thin layer of flour across the sand.

5. Repeat Steps 3 and 4. Put a final layer of sand on top.

6. Hold the sides of the particle board tightly, and push it slowly to the center of the box.

7. In your lab group, discuss factors that could cause mountains to wear down. Write a hypothesis that could be tested with an experiment.

8. Write a procedure for your experiment. Include Safety Alerts.

9. Have your hypothesis, procedure, and Safety Alerts approved by your teacher. Then carry out your experiment. Record your results.

Cleanup/Disposal

See your teacher for cleanup instructions.

Mountain Building, continued

Analysis

1. What happened to the layers of sand and flour as you pushed on the board? Make a drawing of the mountain you formed and the layers of "rock" inside it.

   _____

   _____

2. What happened when you tested your hypothesis?

   _____

   _____

Conclusions

1. What do the sand and flour layers represent?

   _____

   _____

2. Was your hypothesis supported by the results of your investigation? Explain why or why not.

   _____

   _____

Explore Further

Look for examples of the processes you modeled in the area where you live.

   _____

   _____

   _____

   _____

Express Lab 3

Use with Express Lab 3, page 84

Materials   aquarium with fish

pencil

paper

Procedure

1. Observe the fish tank in your classroom.

2. Draw all the parts of the fishes environment.

3. Label each item as biotic or abiotic.

Analysis

1. What are some ways that the abiotic factors in the fish's environment affect the biotic factors?

    _____

    _____

2. Describe the environment of the fish in terms of the atmosphere, lithosphere, and hydrosphere.

    _____

    _____

The Effect of Temperature on Yeast Fermentation

Yeasts are living things. Like all living things, they need food to make energy. The energy-making process in yeast is called fermentation. Certain requirements must be met for fermentation to occur. These requirements include the abiotic factors of food, water, and temperature. A change in these factors may slow or even stop fermentation.

In this lab, you will study the effects of temperature variations on yeast fermentation.

Materials

safety goggles	graduated cylinder
lab coat or apron	tap water
microwave oven	microwavable cup
4 1-liter plastic bottles	package of baker's yeast
4 round balloons	tablespoon
sugar	marking pen
ice	

Procedure

1. Put on safety goggles and a lab coat or apron.

2. Label four plastic bottles A, B, C, and D.

3. Place 100 mL of ice water in Bottle A, 100 mL of room-temperature water in Bottle B, and 100 mL of warm tap water in Bottle C.

4. Use the microwave to heat some water in a cup to boiling. Place 100 mL of this water in Bottle D.

5. Place a tablespoon of sugar in all four bottles.

6. Add a tablespoon of dry yeast to each bottle. Immediately stretch a balloon over the mouth of each bottle.

7. Observe the size of each balloon over the next 15 minutes. Record your observations in your notebook.

Cleanup/Disposal

Follow your teacher's instructions for cleanup and disposal.

The Effect of Temperature on Yeast Fermentation, continued

Analysis

1. Which balloon inflated the most?

_____

_____

2. Which balloon inflated the least?

_____

_____

3. What abiotic factor was different among the four bottles?

_____

Conclusions

1. What evidence did you have that fermentation was occurring?

_____

_____

2. Describe the best temperature for yeast fermentation.

_____

_____

Explore Further

Repeat this experiment by varying the amount of sugar placed in
each bottle and keeping the temperature the same.

_____

_____

_____

_____

The Energy Pyramid

Use with Investigation 3, pages 102–103

An energy pyramid shows how the amount of available energy decreases as it moves through trophic levels. In this lab, you will track this energy. You will use money to represent the energy as it moves between levels.

Materials   data table

pencil

$300 of play money

calculator

Procedure

1. Form a group of four students. Choose someone to be the sun bank, the grass bank, the rabbit bank, and the fox bank.

2. Make a data table like the one below.

Trophic level	Amount earned	Amount spent	Amount saved	Number of organisms
Grass				
Rabbits				
Foxes				

3. The grass bank represents 300 grass plants. Each plant makes $1 a day through photosynthesis. Have the sun bank pay $300 to the grass bank. Record this amount in your data table under "Amount earned." The grass bank does not lose money in this transfer, since no energy is "spent." Record the same amount under "Amount saved."

4. Have the grass bank pay the rabbit bank the money it has saved. Record this in the data table under "Amount earned." According to the 10 percent rule, the rabbit bank "spends" 90 percent of this money right away. Record this amount in your table. Then calculate and record the total amount that is saved.

The Energy Pyramid, continued

5. A rabbit needs $2 a day to survive. Calculate how many rabbits can be supported by the amount of money saved in the rabbit bank. Record this number in your data table.

6. Have the rabbit bank pay the fox bank the money it has saved. Record this amount, the amount that is spent (remember the 10 percent rule), and how much is saved.

7. A fox needs $3 a day to survive. Calculate how many foxes can be supported by the amount of money saved in the fox bank. Record this number in your data table.

Cleanup/Disposal

Put away the materials and make sure your lab area is clean.

Analysis

1. How much money is remaining at the end of the lab?

_____

2. What does the money that was spent represent?

_____

Conclusions

1. What happened to the grass plants that provided energy for the rabbits? How will this affect the energy available the next day?

_____

_____

2. If the rabbit population grew very large, how would other organisms be affected?

_____

_____

Explore Further

Calculate how many more grass plants and rabbits would be needed to support 10 more foxes.

_____

_____

Graphing a Predator-Prey Relationship

Animals must eat plants or other animals to survive. An animal that hunts and eats another is called a predator. The animal the predator eats is called the prey. The size of each population is controlled by the other. As a result, the whole ecosystem benefits from this relationship.

In this lab, you will make a line graph to illustrate a predator-prey relationship.

Materials   graph paper
colored pencils
calculator (optional)

Procedure

1. The data table below shows changes in the populations of wolves and rabbits over a 10-year period.

Year	1	2	3	4	5	6	7	8	9	10
Rabbit	50	300	150	100	450	200	150	200	350	50
Wolf	100	200	250	50	200	350	300	100	200	150

2. Graph the data in the data table.

   A Number the years, 1 through 10, across the bottom of your graph paper.

   B Number the population size on the left side. Let each line represent 50 individuals.

   C Label the bottom of your graph "Years." Label the left side of your graph "Population."

3. Plot the rabbit data in red.

4. Plot the wolf data in green.

Graphing a Predator-Prey Relationship, continued

Analysis

1. What year was the rabbit population the highest?

_____

2. What year was the wolf population the highest?

_____

3. Which years was the rabbit population the lowest?

_____

Conclusions

1. What happens to the rabbit population when there are few wolves?

_____

2. What happens to the wolf population when there are few rabbits?

_____

3. What causes the wolf population to decrease?

_____

_____

Explore Further

Research the Internet to find other predator-prey graphs. How are they
similar to yours? How are they different?

_____

_____

_____

_____

Predator-Prey Interactions
Use with Discovery Investigation 3, pages 110–111

All predators and prey have ways to be successful in their environments. Hawks, for example, have sharp beaks and talons to help them catch prey. Rabbits move quickly to escape capture. Some predators and prey use camouflage to survive. In this lab, you will explore how these factors benefit predators and prey.

Materials   variety of plastic utensils

tweezers

toothpicks

chopsticks

watch, stopwatch, or timer

multicolored pasta

Procedure

1. Your teacher will lead you to an outdoor site. Note the environmental conditions around you. **Safety Alert: Be careful around plants and animals. Let your teacher know if you are bitten, scratched, or stung.**

2. The colored pasta represents the prey. Your teacher will provide a selection of tools to "capture" prey. Examine these tools.

3. Work in pairs. With your partner, write a hypothesis that describes how successful a "predator" will be at capturing the pasta "prey." Your hypothesis can include information on the type of pasta, the environment, or the tools used.

4. Test your hypothesis. Spread out the pasta while one partner is not looking. The "predator" should choose a tool and capture as much "prey" as possible.

5. Stop the predator after 30 seconds. Count the number of prey captured successfully.

6. Repeat the process five times. Vary the tool used and the test site. Record your data.

Cleanup/Disposal
Before returning to the classroom, clean up your materials. Wash your hands afterward.

Predator-Prey Interactions, continued

Analysis

1. What was your hypothesis?

_____

_____

2. Was your hypothesis supported by the data you collected?
Explain your answer.

_____

_____

Conclusions

1. How did the tools of the "predator" affect its success at predation?

_____

_____

2. How did the color of the "prey" affect success?

_____

_____

3. How did the environment affect success?

_____

_____

Explore Further

Choose a different type of prey and different tools. Write a
hypothesis with these new factors and test them.

_____

_____

_____

_____

Express Lab 4

Use with Express Lab 4, page 127

Materials   paper
pencil

Procedure

1. Work with a partner to determine three of your genetic traits.

2. Make a table like the one shown below.

Name	Eye color (light or dark)	Hair (curly or straight)	Little finger (straight or bent)

3. Record your traits in the table.

4. List all the different combination of the three traits that are possible.

5. Count the total number of classmates with each combination.

Analysis

1. How many combinations of these three traits are possible?

_____

_____

2. How many students had each type of combination?

_____

_____

Variety Within a Population

Organisms of the same species are not all alike. For example, all zebras may seem to look the same. However, each zebra is different. No two zebras have exactly the same pattern of stripes. Differences within a population are known as genetic diversity. Differences can give one organism an advantage over another. Adaptations, for example, help an organism survive in its environment.

In this lab, you will explore differences within populations.

Materials   metric ruler
10 green bean pods
10 pinto bean seeds

Procedure

Part A: Differences in Bean Coats

1. Draw Data Table A on your paper.

2. Examine the 10 pinto beans. Look for differences in color: light, medium, and dark brown.

3. Group the seeds by their color.

4. Record the number of each color in Data Table A.

Data Table A

Color	Light Brown	Medium Brown	Dark Brown
Number of Beans			

Variety Within a Population, continued

Part B: Differences in Bean Length

1. Draw Data Table B on your paper.

2. Use the metric ruler to measure the length of each green bean in millimeters.

3. Record your measurements in Data Table B.

Data Table B

Bean	Measurement in mm	Bean	Measurement in mm
1		6	
2		7	
3		8	
4		9	
5		10	

Analysis

1. What color were most of the pinto beans?

   _____

2. Were most of the green beans long or short?

   _____

Conclusions

1. Describe the differences you found in bean color.

   _____

2. How might dark color be an advantage to a bean? _____

   _____

3. How might a long bean have an advantage over a short one? _____

   _____

Explore Further

   Graph your measurements for bean length.

Modeling Natural Selection
Use with Investigation 4, pages 141–142

Natural selection acts on the genetic diversity in the populations of a species. Different combinations of genes carried by individuals provide advantages or disadvantages in a given environment. An individual's genes are passed on if the individual survives long enough to reproduce. The environment determines which combination of genes are the most successful. How does natural selection work? You will model the process in this lab.

Materials   paper

pencil

20 dried white beans

20 dried black beans

20 dried kidney beans

sheet of black construction paper

sheet of white construction paper

Procedure

1. Make a data table like the one shown below.

Environmental conditions	Number of white beans remaining	Number of black beans remaining	Number of kidney beans remaining
Black paper			
White paper			

2. Scatter 10 of each bean type on black paper.

3. Close your eyes. After five seconds, open your eyes and pick up the first bean you see. Repeat until you have 10 beans.

4. Record your observations in your data table.

5. Repeat Steps 2–5 using white construction paper.

Modeling Natural Selection, continued

Cleanup/Disposal

Before leaving the lab, return your materials and wash your hands.

Analysis

1. How many kidney beans were left on the black paper?

_____

_____

2. How was the number of remaining beans different for each paper color?

_____

_____

Conclusions

1. What would eventually happen if you continued the selection process using only the beans remaining on the paper?

_____

_____

2. How does this activity model natural selection?

_____

_____

Explore Further

Repeat the investigation using different colors of paper and different combinations of beans.

_____

_____

_____

_____

Symbiosis

Symbiosis is a close relationship between two organisms. When the relationship is good for both, it is called mutualism. When the relationship is good for one but bad for the other, it is called parasitism. When a relationship is good for one and the other is not affected, it is called commensalism. In these relationships, organisms are dependant on each other in many ways.

In this lab, you will observe a symbiotic relationship that includes algae and fungi.

Materials
     safety goggles
     lab coat or apron
     sample of a lichen soaking in a bowl of water
     compound light microscope
     microscope slide
     cover slip
     2 forceps
     eyedropper

Procedure

1. Put on safety goggles and a lab coat or apron.

2. Use the forceps to pick up a small sample of lichen. Your sample should be no larger than the head of a pin.

3. Place the lichen on the microscope slide. Use the other forcep to tear the lichen tissue into smaller pieces.

4. Use the eyedropper to add a drop of water to the pieces of lichen.

5. Place the cover slip over the lichen.

6. Position the slide and cover slip on the microscope stage. Turn on the light.

7. Focus the microscope on low power. Switch to high power and focus again.

8. In your notebook, draw what you see.

Symbiosis, continued

Analysis

1. Describe what you saw under the microscope.

    _____

    _____

2. Lichen are made up of fungi, algae, and cyanobacteria. Label some of
    the algae cells in your drawing.

Conclusions

1. What is symbiosis?

    _____

2. How do you think the algae benefit in this relationship?

    _____

3. How do you think the fungi benefit from this relationship?

    _____

4. What kind of symbiotic relationship do the fungi and algae share?

    _____

Explore Further

Research two other symbiotic relationships. Write a brief description of
each relationship.

_____

_____

_____

_____

Conducting a Biodiversity Survey
Use with Discovery Investigation 4, pages 155–156

Think of a time when you walked across a lawn or a field at school. You might have noticed just one kind of living thing, grass. Is that all that is there? What diversity of life is found under your feet and above your head? Find out in this lab.

Materials   latex gloves   4 dowels or tent pegs

field notebook   magnifying glass

4 1-meter pieces of string   plastic bag

Procedure

1. Form a group of three students. Decide who will be a data recorder, an animal surveyor, and a plant surveyor. A surveyor is someone who surveys, or examines, the land.

2. At the survey site, put on protective gloves if you are a surveyor. Lay the 1-meter pieces of string in a square on the ground. You may secure the ends to wooden dowels or tent pegs.

3. Look for and record every kind of plant or animal inside the square. Use descriptions or draw pictures if you do not know the name of something. Also record any signs of living things, such as seeds or animal waste.

4. In your lab group, discuss factors that affect biodiversity in different areas. Write a hypothesis that could be tested with an experiment. Include the way you will measure biodiversity. Your experiment should use sampling.

5. Write a procedure for your experiment. Include Safety Alerts.

6. Have your hypothesis, procedure, and Safety Alerts approved by your teacher. Then carry out your experiment. Record the results.

Cleanup/Disposal

Make sure to collect all materials when you leave your survey site. Wash your hands with warm, soapy water.

Conducting a Biodiversity Survey, continued

Analysis

1. Work with your group to summarize your data in a table or chart.

_____

_____

2. How does biodiversity vary among the sites?

_____

_____

Conclusions

1. Was your hypothesis supported by the results of your experiment? Explain.

_____

_____

2. How does the amount of human activity affect biodiversity?

_____

_____

Explore Further

Conduct biodiversity surveys in other locations, such as your backyard or a local park.

_____

_____

_____

_____

Express Lab 5

Use with Express Lab 5, page 168

Materials   flashlight
globe
cash register paper
toilet paper tube
masking tape

Procedure

1. Tape a strip of cash register paper on a globe from a little below the equator to the North Pole.

2. Tape the end of a toilet paper tube to the flashlight so that the beam of light will be better focused.

3. Hold the flashlight about 30 cm away from the globe. Turn it on and shine it directly at the equator.

4. On the paper, have a partner draw the shape of the area the light shines on.

5. Move the flashlight up so that it shines on the middle latitudes. Then move it so it shines near the North Pole. Repeat Step 4 each time.

Analysis

1. How do the shapes of the lighted areas change?

_____

_____

2. The flashlight represents the sun. How do you think the way the sun shines on Earth affects temperatures in different places?

_____

_____

Salinity and Density
Use with Investigation 5, pages 170–171

Saltwater and freshwater biomes have different levels of salinity. Another difference between these biomes is the density of the water. In this lab, you will compare water that has different levels of salinity. You will observe how salinity and density are related and how density affects flotation.

Materials   safety goggles

lab coat or apron

2 plastic jars

water

table salt

stir stick

spoon

2 eggs

Procedure

1. Put on safety goggles and a lab coat or apron.

2. Fill both jars about two-thirds full of water. Add about 2 teaspoons of salt to one of the jars. Stir until the salt is dissolved in the water. **Safety Alert: Do not taste or drink the saltwater solution.**

3. Using a spoon, gently place an egg in the freshwater. **Safety Alert: Be careful when handling the eggs.** Observe and record what happens.

4. Gently place the second egg in the salt water. Observe and record what happens.

Cleanup/Disposal

Before leaving the classroom, clean up your materials. Wash your hands afterward.

Salinity and Density, continued

Analysis

1. What happened to the egg in the freshwater?

_____

_____

2. What happened to the egg in the salt water?

_____

_____

3. Which type of water has the higher salinity?

_____

_____

4. Density is measured by the weight of a given volume. Which has the higher density, freshwater or salt water?

_____

_____

Conclusions

1. Explain how the different salinities and densities of the water affected the eggs.

_____

_____

2. How might a change in salinity affect life in an aquatic biome?

_____

_____

Explore Further

Add one ice cube at a time to a jar of freshwater. Record your observations. What can you conclude about the effect of temperature on water density?

_____

_____

_____

_____

Grassland Erosion

Use with Discovery Investigation 5, pages 189–190

Rainfall and streams can cause soils to erode. This can harm habitats on land and in the water. Planting grasses and other plants keeps the soils from washing away. In this lab, you will test how well different plants prevent land from eroding.

Materials   2 aluminum pie plates

soil

grass seeds

radish seeds

balance or scale

water

watering can

Procedure

1. In a small group, review the characteristics of grassland biomes. Note the type of vegetation and the amount of rainfall.

2. Write out a procedure for comparing how well certain plants prevent grasslands from eroding.

3. Have your procedure approved by your teacher. Include Safety Alerts and a data table with headings.

4. Label the two pie plates. Fill each with a layer of soil, then plant grass seeds in one and radish seeds in the other. Place the pie plates in a sunny area.

5. Wait a few weeks for the plants to grow, watering them regularly. Then begin your experiment.

6. Follow your procedure for testing how well different types of plants prevent erosion. Record your results in your data table.

Cleanup/Disposal

Follow your teacher's instructions for disposing of your soil and plants.

Grassland Erosion, continued

Analysis

1. Which plant did the best job of preventing erosion? Explain.

   _____

   _____

2. How could you change the experiment to compare erosion from wind?

   _____

   _____

Conclusions

1. What types of plants do you think landscapers might plant on a hill?

   _____

   _____

2. How do the roots of different plants affect erosion?

   _____

   _____

   _____

Explore Further

Use your procedure to measure the erosion of bare soil with no plants.
Compare the measurements with your results above.

   _____

   _____

   _____

   _____

Staying Warm in the Tundra

Animals that live in the tundra have special adaptations for staying warm. Environmentalists have noticed that many tundra animals are larger than their warm-weather cousins. Tundra hares, for example, are much taller and heavier than desert hares. Artic lemmings, relatives of mice, are bigger than temperate biome mice. Large size may be an advantage to animals in cold-weather climates.

In this lab activity, you will find out how size affects conservation of body heat.

Materials   safety goggles
lab coat or apron
2 thermometers
small plastic bowl
large plastic bowl
access to hot tap water
access to cold weather outdoors or a refrigerator

Procedure

1. Put on safety goggles and a lab coat or apron.

2. Half-fill both bowls with hot tap water.

3. Place a thermometer in each bowl. After one minute, read the temperature on each thermometer. Record the temperatures on a piece of paper as "starting temperatures."

4. Place both bowls in a cold place (outdoors or in a refrigerator) for 20 minutes. Leave the thermometers in the bowls.

5. Read the temperature on each thermometer. Record the temperatures on a piece of paper as "final temperatures."

6. For each bowl, subtract the final temperature from the starting temperature. Record the difference on your paper.

Staying Warm in the Tundra, continued

Cleanup/Disposal

Follow your teacher's instructions for cleanup and disposal of materials.

Analysis

1. How much did the water cool in the small bowl?

_____

2. How much did the water cool in the large bowl?

_____

Conclusions

1. Explain the relationship of the size of a bowl of water and heat retention.

_____

_____

2. Based on your results, which animal would stay warm the longest: a small one or a large one?

_____

_____

3. What is one reason that animals living in the tundra are are larger than their relatives in warm-weather climates?

_____

_____

Explore Further

Many tundra animals have short legs and ears. Repeat the experiment using latex gloves and round balloons as containers. Find out whether the fingers of a glove hold heat as well as the round balloon. Relate your findings to the body shapes of tundra animals.

_____

_____

_____

_____

Desert Animals Conserve Water

Deserts are incredibly dry biomes. Desert plants and animals have very little access to water. To survive, they must conserve as much water as possible.

In this lab activity, you will design an adaptation to help a "desert organism" conserve water.

Materials   safety goggles   masking tape or labels

lab coat or apron   pen

2 sponges   additional materials for

2 aluminum pie plates   conserving water: paper, waxed

scale or triple-beam balance   paper, aluminum foil, petroleum

access to water   jelly, cotton balls, feathers, soil,

access to a heat lamp   leaves, blades of grasses

or an open area outdoors

Procedure: Day 1

1. Copy the data table on a piece of paper.

Sponge	Weight on Day 1	Weight on Day 2	Difference in Day 1 and Day 2 weights
A			
B			

2. Put on safety goggles and a lab coat or apron.

3. Use the pen and masking tape or labels to label one pie plate as A. Label the other pie plate as B.

4. Dip the sponges in water. Squeeze the sponges slightly to remove any excess water. These wet sponges represent desert animals.

5. Place each wet sponge in an aluminum pie plate.

6. Weigh each sponge and pie plate. Record the weights on the data table under "Weight on Day 1."

7. Examine the materials for conserving water.

Desert Animals Conserve Water, continued

8. Select one of these materials. On your paper, write a plan for using this material to prevent water loss in Sponge A.

9. Carry out your plan.

10. Sponge A represents an organism with a water-conserving adaptation. Sponge B represents an organism without a water-conserving adaptation. Place both sponges (in their pie plates) in an open area or under a heat lamp for 24 hours.

Procedure: Day 2

1. Remove any material from Sponge A that you added on the previous day.

2. Weigh Sponge A and its pie plate. Record the weight on the data table under "Weight on Day 2."

3. Repeat Step 2 for Sponge B.

4. For each sponge, subtract the Day 2 weight from the Day 1 weight. Record your answers on the data table under "Difference in Day 1 and Day 2 weights."

5. Compare your results to those of your classmates.

Analysis

1. Did the material you selected help Sponge A conserve water?

_____

_____

2. In this experiment, Sponge B is the control. Why does this experiment need a control?

_____

_____

Desert Animals Conserve Water, continued

Conclusions

1. Why do desert animals need adaptations for saving water?

_____

_____

2. Examine the list of plant adaptations in the chart. Put an X in the second column if the adaptation helps plants conserve water.

Can carry out photosynthesis	
Thin thorns replace wide leaves	
Leaves have a waxy coating	
Leaves have openings to take in carbon dioxide gas	

Explore Further

Design an "ideal" desert plant. Explain all of the adaptations your plant has for conserving water.

_____

_____

_____

_____

Express Lab 6

Use with Express Lab 6, page 220

Materials   paper
pencil
dried beans

Procedure

1. Create two piles with two beans each. Label each pile. One will be the Arithmetic Growth pile. The other will be the Exponential Growth pile.

2. Create a data table to record the number of beans in each pile. Record your starting numbers.

3. Add two more beans to the Arithmetic Growth pile. Double the number of beans in the Exponential Growth pile.

4. Record the new totals.

5. Repeat Steps 3 and 4 four more times.

Analysis

1. What do the beans in each group represent?

_____

_____

2. Which population grew the fastest?

_____

_____

3. How could this activity be changed to model real population growth?

_____

_____

Modeling Exponential Growth

When a population increases, it may show linear or exponential growth. In linear growth, the population increases by a constant number. For example, a population begins with 100 individuals and increases by 10 each year. At the end of one year, the population contains 110 individuals. After 2 years, it has 120 individuals, and after 3 years, 130 individuals. In exponential growth, the existing population doubles. A population of 100 individuals would soar to 200 after one year, 400 after the second year, and 800 after the third year.

In this lab activity, you will model exponential population growth.

Materials   safety goggles

lab coat or apron

plastic container with lid (large enough to hold 150 six-sided number cubes)

150 six-sided number cubes

graph paper

Procedure

1. Make a data table like the one below. Extend your data table so that it has 30 rows.

Throw number (Year)	Number of births (*Nb*)	Number of deaths (*Nd*)	Population size	Growth rate (Change per year)
0				
1				
2				
3				
⋮				
30				

Modeling Exponential Growth, continued

2. Put on safety goggles and a lab coat or apron.

3. In this activity, each six-sided number cube represents one person. Each throw of a six-sided cube represents one year.

4. Place 10 six-sided number cubes in the plastic container. These cubes represent the population in Year 0. The population of Year 0 has already been recorded on the data table.

5. Cover the plastic container with a lid and shake.

6. Open the plastic container and pour the contents onto your desk or table.

7. Count the number of "ones" that were thrown on the six-sided cubes. Ones represent deaths in the population. Record the number in the column titled "Number of deaths (Nd)" for Year 1.

8. Count the total number of threes and sixes that were thrown. Record the total number of threes and sixes in the column titled "Number of births (Nb)" for Year 1.

9. Subtract Nd from Nb. Record this number in the column titled "Growth rate."

   A If the growth rate is a negative number, remove that many cubes from your population. Count the number of cubes that remain in the plastic container. Record the number of remaining cubes in the column titled "Population" for Year 1.

   B If the number is positive, add that many cubes to the plastic container. Record the size of the new population in the column titled "Population" for Year 1.

   C If the number is zero, there was no change in population size. Write 10 in the column titled "Number of Cubes" for Year 1.

10. Repeat the above procedure until the total population exceeds 100.

11. Make a line graph of the population for each year.

Cleanup/Disposal

Follow your teacher's instructions for cleanup and disposal of materials.

Modeling Exponential Growth, continued

Analysis

1. In what year was the population the lowest? _____

2. In what year was the population the greatest? _____

3. In what year did the population increase the most? _____

Conclusions

1. How many times greater was the birth rate than the death rate?

    _____

2. Compare the graph you created to the graph in Figure 6.1.1
    on page 217 of your textbook. How is your graph similar?
    How is it different?

    _____

    _____

    _____

Explore Further

Population size is not the only thing that increases exponentially.
Research other things that grow at an exponential rate.

Sampling Populations

It is difficult to determine the size of a population in its natural environment. Scientists use a technique called sampling to help them estimate populations. In sampling, every organism in the population does not have to be counted.

In this lab activity, you will use sampling to estimate the size of a population.

Materials   safety goggles
    lab coat or apron
    desktop or table top
    bag of colored beads
    small paper cup
    metric ruler

    top of a round plastic
      container with the center
      cut out to make a ring
    water-soluble marker
    calculator

Procedure

1. Put on safety goggles and a lab coat or apron.

2. Use the paper cup to scoop up a few beads. These beads represent a population. Do not count the beads in your cup.

3. Pour the beads onto your desktop. Be careful not to let any fall off.

4. Without looking at the desktop, drop the plastic ring over the population.

5. Count the number of beads that are within the ring. Record this number in your notebook.

6. Use a marker to put a small mark on each bead within the ring.

7. Remove the ring and repeat Steps 4 through 6 four more times. Only count the beads that do not have marks.

8. Total all counts. This total represents the estimated size of your population.

9. Count the beads on your desktop. This total represents the actual size of your population. Return the beads to the bag.

Cleanup/Disposal

Follow your teacher's instructions for cleanup and disposal of materials.

Sampling Populations, continued

Analysis

1. What was the estimated size of your population?

   _____

2. What was the actual size of your population?

   _____

Conclusions

1. When counting samples, why did you not count the beads that were marked?

   _____

   _____

2. Beads cannot move around. However, animals are very mobile. How might your count have been different if your beads were mobile?

   _____

3. Why might a scientist need to know the size of a population?

   _____

   _____

   _____

Explore Further

Use this sampling technique to count a population of plants.
Use a plastic hoop as your ring.

Making an Age-Structure Histogram

Use with Investigation 6, pages 233–234

A population's age structure is the number of males and females in each age group. A bar graph called a histogram is used to display age-structure data. You will make an age-structure histogram in this lab. But first, you will collect data on the age structure of a population.

Materials   paper

pencil

population data

calculator

ruler

Procedure

1. Collect data on the ages of your living family members. Include parents, siblings, cousins, aunts, uncles, grandparents, and great-grandparents.

2. Make a data table like the one below on your paper. Include a row for every 10 years of age up to 81+.

Age group	Males		Females	
	Number	**Percent**	**Number**	**Percent**
0–10				
11–20				
21–30				
31–40				
41–50				
51–60				
61–70				
81+				

3. Enter the pooled numbers of males and females in each age group.

Making an Age-Structure Histogram, continued

4. Calculate what percent of each age group are males and females. Enter this data.

5. Begin building a histogram. Label each age group, starting with the youngest group on the bottom. Arrange your labels as shown in the diagram.

6. Draw a bar that represents all the people in the 0–10 age group. Draw a vertical line that divides the bar into two parts, one for males and one for females.

7. Repeat Step 6 for each age group. Place each bar on top of the last. Line up the dividing lines to make one solid vertical line.

Cleanup/Disposal

Before leaving the lab, put away all your materials.

Analysis

1. Which age groups have more males, and which have more females?

_____

2. Describe the general shape of the histogram you created.

_____

Conclusions

1. How do the life expectancies of males and females compare? _____

2. How does your histogram compare with the one for the United States?

_____

_____

_____

_____

_____

Explore Further

Make age-structure histograms for other populations.

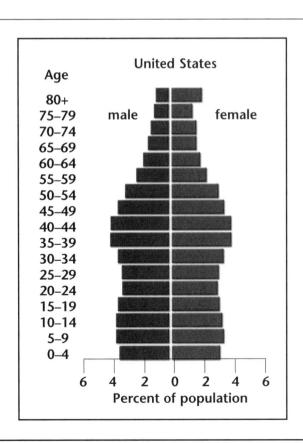

Analyze Your Trash

Use with Discovery Investigation 6, pages 241–242

If people reduce the amount of waste they produce, they also reduce their environmental impact. How much waste do you produce from consumption? Are there ways you could produce less? To answer these questions, you need to know what kinds of materials you throw away. In this lab, you will analyze household trash. You will then use the data to make predictions and propose solutions.

Materials
    safety goggles

    lab coat or apron

    gloves

    spring scale

    plastic grocery bags

    marker

    1 day's household trash, minus food wastes

    calculator

Procedure

1. In a small group, discuss the kinds of materials that you throw away. Write a hypothesis in which you predict the mount of garbage produced in a typical household each day. You will test your hypothesis with an experiment using the materials listed.

2. Write a procedure for your experiment. Include Safety Alerts for handling garbage.

3. Have your hypothesis, procedure, and Safety Alerts approved by your teacher.

4. Carry out your experiment. Record your results.

Cleanup/Disposal

Before you leave the lab, be sure your work area is clean. Wash your hands thoroughly.

Analyze Your Trash, continued

Analysis

1. What is the average amount of trash thrown away by each person in the household?

_____

_____

2. Make a circle graph of your group's data.

3. How does the makeup of your group's trash compare with that of other groups?

_____

_____

Conclusions

1. At this rate, how much trash would each person throw away in a month? A year?

_____

_____

2. How can you explain any differences in the groups' trash?

_____

_____

3. What are three things you could do to produce less trash?

_____

_____

Explore Further

Analyze the contents of the trash in the classroom or the trash from an office.

_____

_____

_____

_____

Express Lab 7

Use with Express Lab 7, page 252

Materials tennis ball

Procedure

1. Place the ball on top of a desk. Push the ball just enough so that it falls off the edge of the desk.

2. Hold the ball at shoulder height, then drop it.

3. Hold the ball at waist height, then drop it.

Analysis

1. When does the ball display kinetic energy?

  _____

  _____

2. When does the ball display potential energy?

  _____

  _____

3. At what point does the ball have the most potential energy?

  _____

  _____

Designing a Solar House

Most of us heat our homes and fuel our vehicles with fossil fuels. Oil, coal, and natural gas are examples of fossil fuels. All fossil fuels are nonrenewable and their supplies are dwindling. Scientists are looking for ways to use renewable energy sources. One of the most promising renewable energy sources is the sun.

In this lab, you will design and build a model solar house.

Materials

safety goggles	watch or clock
lab coat or apron	access to a sunny location
shoe box with lid	some of the following
scissors	materials: rocks,
plastic wrap	containers of water,
thermometer	black paint, white paint,
tape	colored paper, cardboard,
metric ruler	foil, soil, wood pieces,
	foam peanuts

Procedure

1. Put on safety goggles and a lab coat or apron.

2. Draw a data table like the one below on a sheet of paper.

	Start	**5 min**	**10 min**	**15 min**	**20 min**	**25 min**	**30 min**
A							
B							

3. The shoe box will be your model house. Your first task is to find out how easily the house warms.

4. Cut out two windows. Each window should be 5 cm x 5 cm.

5. Cover the windows with plastic wrap. Secure the plastic wrap with tape.

6. Place a thermometer in the model. Position the thermometer so that it can be read through one of the windows. Place the lid on the box.

Designing a Solar House, continued

7. Place your solar house in the sun. Read the temperature. Record the temperature in Row A under "Start."

8. Record the temperature every 5 minutes for 30 minutes.

9. Examine the materials provided. Select one material that you could use to make the model warmer.

10. Use the material to change your model so that it will become warmer.

11. Repeat Steps 5 through 7. Record the temperatures in Row B of the data table.

Analysis

1. Why was it important to collect the information that you recorded in Row A of the data table?

_____

2. What material did you use to change your model? _____
Why did you choose this material?

_____

Conclusions

1. Compare your results with those of your classmates. What materials were best at holding solar heat in the model?

_____

2. Suggest some ways to increase the use of solar energy in your own home.

_____

_____

Explore Further

Find out what kinds of house designs take advantage of solar energy. How do they compare to your model house?

_____

_____

_____

_____

Using Wind Energy to Do Work

Use with Investigation 7, pages 279–280

Wind power is the wind's kinetic energy. Modern wind turbines take this energy and produce electricity. How did early windmills use wind power? Most did work, such as pumping water, which was powered directly by the wind. In this lab, you will model how early windmills worked.

Materials
1- or 2-liter plastic bottle	string
sand	large paperclip
paper	assortment of washers
pencil with an eraser	thumbtack

Procedure

1. Create a pinwheel from a square of stiff paper by cutting diagonally from the corners to the center. Do not cut through the center. Then take the left corner of each triangle formed and fold it into the center. Pin the corners down with a thumbtack pushed into a pencil's eraser.

2. Cut the top half off a 1- or 2-liter bottle. Fill the bottom fourth of the bottle with sand. Punch two holes across from each other in the rim of the bottle. Push the pencil through the holes.

3. Tightly tie or tape one end of the string to the pencil. Bend the paperclip into an S shape and tie one end of it to the other end of the string. Hook a washer on the paperclip.

4. Blow gently until the pinwheel turns and winds up the string.

5. Add another washer to the paperclip and repeat Step 4. Continue adding washers until the pinwheel can no longer lift them without you blowing harder.

6. Add a second student blowing against the pinwheel. Add washers to find out how much weight the pinwheel can lift now.

Cleanup/Disposal

Return the materials and make sure your area is clean before you leave the lab.

Using Wind Energy to Do Work, continued

Analysis

1. How many washers were you able to lift by blowing gently?

_____

_____

2. How many washers were you able to lift with two people blowing?

_____

_____

Conclusions

1. What type of energy makes the pinwheel turn?

_____

_____

2. How does the amount of wind affect the amount of energy that can be produced by the windmill?

_____

_____

3. How can wind be used to make electricity?

_____

_____

Explore Further

Observe two pinwheels of different sizes next to each other in front of a fan. Describe what you observe. How does the size of the pinwheel affect how much work can it do?

_____

_____

_____

_____

Energy-Conserving Insulation

When you feel cold, you put on a sweater or jacket. By doing this you are conserving your heat energy and keeping warm. Do you know how this happens? As you add more layers of clothing, you trap air. Air transfers heat very slowly. That is why air is a very good insulator. Any material that helps conserve heat energy is called an insulator.

In this lab activity, you will test materials to see which one is the best insulator.

Materials

safety goggles

lab coat or apron

coffee can with lid

smaller can (washed, with the lid removed)

outdoor thermometer

nail

heatproof mitt

water

graduated cylinder

hot plate

saucepan

watch or clock

materials to test as insulation: sand, shredded paper, cotton balls, sawdust, feathers, wool, soil, rigid foam, foam packing peanuts, cardboard, thick cloth, faux fur, pebbles

Procedure

1. Put on safety goggles and a lab coat or apron.

2. Use the nail to carefully poke a hole through the center of the plastic coffee can lid.

3. Select one of the materials to test as an insulator. Layer the material on the bottom of the coffee can.

4. Place the smaller can on top of the material inside the coffee can. Add more of the same material around the small can.

5. Make a data table in your notebook like the one below.

Material	Starting temperature	5 minutes	10 minutes	15 minutes	20 minutes	25 minutes	30 minutes

Energy-Conserving Insulation, continued

6. Measure 200 mL of water in the graduated cylinder. Pour the water into the saucepan.

7. Place the saucepan on the hot plate. Heat the water to boiling.

8. Wearing the heatproof mitt, pour the boiling water into the small can. Turn off the hot plate.

9. Quickly place the lid on the coffee can and insert the thermometer through the hole. Position the thermometer so the bulb is in the water but not touching the small can.

10. Read the water temperature and record under "Starting temperature."

11. Read and record the temperature every 5 minutes for 30 minutes.

12. Repeat Steps 3–11 with a different material.

Analysis

1. Calculate the change in temperature over 30 minutes in each test. To do so, subtract your first temperature from your last.

_____

_____

2. Of the materials you tested, which lost the most heat?

_____

_____

Conclusions

1. Which of the materials you tested was the best insulator?

_____

2. How could the results of your test be applied to your everyday life?

_____

_____

Explore Further

Compare your results to others tested by your classmates. Determine which material was the best insulator overall.

How Can You Conserve Energy?

Use with Discovery Investigation 7, pages 285–286

Energy conservation means using energy wisely and efficiently. Conserving energy benefits everyone. It means more fossil fuels are available for the future. It also means less pollution is produced today.

How can you conserve energy in your daily life? In this lab, you will create and follow an energy conservation plan.

Materials   notebook

Procedure

1. Form a small group. Discuss some ways that you can conserve energy at school and at home.

2. Use the library or the Internet to research the conservation methods you discussed. Where possible, find out how much energy each method could save.

3. Create an action plan that you can follow to conserve energy. Include the actions you will take.

4. Have your teacher approve your plan. Then follow your plan for one week.

5. Create a report about your energy conservation methods. Include data on how much energy you saved.

Analysis

1. Were you able to follow your plan? Why or why not?

   _____

   _____

2. What problems, if any, did you have with following your plan?

   _____

   _____

3. How much energy did you conserve?

   _____

   _____

How Can You Conserve Energy?, continued

Conclusions

1. Besides saving energy, in what other ways did your action plan benefit you and the environment?

   _____

   _____

2. How much energy would be saved if everyone in your classroom followed your action plan?

   _____

   _____

3. How much energy would be saved if everyone in the United States followed your action plan?

   _____

   _____

Explore Further

Design a campaign to encourage others to adopt one of your energy conservation methods. Include information that would help others understand how their participation would make a difference.

Express Lab 8

Use with Express Lab 8, page 298

Materials   safety goggles

large glass container (aquarium or baking dish)

rocks, 3–5 cm in diameter

sand

pea gravel

water

ruler

Procedure

1. Put on safety goggles.

2. Spread rocks, 5–10 cm thick, on the bottom of the container.

3. Make a layer of sand, 1–2 cm thick, on top of the rocks.

4. Make an uneven layer of gravel, 1–15 cm thick, on top of the sand.

5. Slowly pour about a liter of water onto different parts of the top layer.

Analysis

1. Which part of the model is the water table?

   _____

   _____

2. How does the water recharge this aquifer?

   _____

   _____

Water Quality Testing

Use with Investigation 8, pages 306–307

How do you know your drinking water is safe to drink? Experts test the water for many contaminants. In this lab, you will test water samples for two different contaminants.

Materials	safety goggles	4 small test tubes and stoppers
	lab coat or apron	test tube rack
	gloves	pH test solution
	tap water	pH color card
	outdoor water	nitrate test solutions #1 and #2
	wax pencil	nitrate color card

Procedure

1. Copy the data table below onto a sheet of paper.

Water source	Kind of test	
	pH	**Nitrate (ppm)**
Tap water		
Outdoor water		

2. Put on safety goggles, a lab coat or apron, and gloves.

3. Place 5 mL of tap water in two test tubes. Label the test tubes A and B using a wax pencil. **Safety Alert: Do not taste any of the water samples.**

4. Add 3–5 drops of the pH test solution to Test Tube A. **Safety Alert: Be careful when handling glassware and chemicals.** Close the test tube with a stopper and gently shake the tube several times.

5. Find the pH of the water by matching the color of the solution to the same color on the pH color card. Record the pH.

6. Add 10 drops of nitrate test solution #1 to Test Tube B. Close the test tube and gently shake it several times.

Water Quality Testing, continued

7. Shake the bottle of nitrate test solution #2 forcefully for 30 seconds. Then add 10 drops of this solution to Test Tube B. Close the test tube again, and shake it forcefully for 1 minute. Let the test tube stand in the test tube rack for 5 minutes.

8. Find the amount of nitrate in the water in parts per million (ppm) by matching the color of the solution to the same color on the nitrate color card. Record the amount of nitrate.

9. Repeat Steps 3–8 for the outdoor water sample.

Cleanup/Disposal

Before you leave the lab, be sure your work area is clean. Wash your hands thoroughly.

Analysis

1. Summarize the results of your tests.

_____

_____

2. How do the two water samples compare?

_____

_____

Conclusions

1. Which water sample would be safest for aquatic life?

_____

_____

2. Can the water you tested be considered safe to drink? Explain.

_____

_____

Explore Further

Test more water samples from different sources such as a creek, a lake, rainwater, and different brands of bottled water.

Operation Oil Spill

In industrialized nations, cars, trucks, and buses are common forms of transportation. All of these vehicles depend on oil. Most oil is drilled offshore then transported to the areas where it is used. Tanker ships and long pipelines are two ways to move oil. The processes of transporting and drilling for oil can lead to oil spills. These spills can destroy fishing grounds, spoil beaches, and kill marine animals. Cleaning up these spills is a difficult job. An oil spill is one of the most destructive forms of water pollution.

In this lab activity, you will compare methods of cleaning up oil spills.

Materials   safety goggles   feathers (to represent marine birds)

lab coat or apron   several of the following items:

shallow pan   spoons, craft sticks, toothpicks,

100 mL vegetable oil   nets, straws, plastic wrap, foil,

water   plastic foam peanuts, paper bags,

sand   cotton balls, nylon hose, sponges,

small rocks or gravel   paper towels, coffee filters, cloth,

pipe cleaners (to represent   sawdust, liquid detergent
   marine mammals)

Procedure

1. Make a copy of the following table in your notebook.

2. Put on safety goggles and a lab coat or apron.

3. In the shallow pan, construct a "beach" and an "ocean." To do so:

   a. Place some sand in one end of the pan.

   b. Add a few rocks, a feather, and a pipe cleaner to your beach.

   c. Slowly pour water into the pan until your ocean is about halfway up the beach.

4. Pour a spoonful of oil onto the surface of the water.

5. Pour a small amount of oil over the rocks, feather, and pipe cleaner.

6. Select five items to use as your cleanup materials.

Operation Oil Spill, continued

Material	Contained spill	Water cleanup and recovery	Shore cleanup	Wildlife cleanup

7. Choose one of the five items you selected. Use it to clean up the oil spill. For each of the categories in the table, rate this item's effectiveness as poor, average, good, or excellent.

8. Repeat Step 7 with the other four items you selected.

Cleanup/Disposal
Follow your teacher's instructions for cleanup and disposal of materials.

Analysis

1. Which item was the easiest to clean: the feather, rocks, or pipe cleaner? _____ Which was the most difficult? _____

2. Which item was the best at cleaning the beach? _____ Which was the worst? _____

3. Which item was the best at removing the oil from the water? _____

Operation Oil Spill, continued

Conclusions

1. Was it possible to completely clean the water, shore, and animals?
   Explain your answer.

   _____

   _____

   _____

2. How might the cleanup of a real oil spill be different from your model?

   _____

   _____

3. How might the cleanup of a real oil spill impact plant and animal life?

   _____

   _____

Explore Further

Research a real oil spill, like the *Exxon Valdez* accident, and describe
the cleanup methods used.

_____

_____

_____

_____

Testing Groundwater

Use with Discovery Investigation 8, pages 314–315

Surface water soaks through one or more layers of soil and rock as it becomes groundwater. As water moves through the ground, soil and rock filter out some pollutants. How well do these materials remove nitrates? Find out by designing and conducting an experiment.

Materials	safety goggles	nitrate color card
	lab coat or apron	soil
	gloves	sand
	outdoor water	gravel
	2 small test tubes and stoppers	filter paper
	test tube rack	funnel
	nitrate test solutions #1 and #2	jars

Procedure

1. In your lab group, discuss the kinds of pollutants that are found in water. Also discuss the kind of soil that is found in your area.

2. Write a hypothesis about how well different soil materials filter out pollutants. This hypothesis should be able to be tested with an experiment that uses the materials listed here.

3. Write a procedure for your experiment. Include Safety Alerts.

4. Have your hypothesis, procedure, and Safety Alerts approved by your teacher. Then carry out your experiment. Record your results.

Cleanup/Disposal

Before you leave the lab, be sure your work area is clean. Wash your hands thoroughly.

Testing Groundwater, continued

Analysis

1. Which kind of material was easiest for water to filter through?

_____

_____

2. What other differences do you notice in the water that has filtered through soil?

_____

_____

Conclusions

1. Which kind of material best filtered nitrates out of the water?

_____

_____

2. Think about the soil types in your area. How well would they filter nitrates out of water?

_____

_____

Explore Further

Repeat your experiment using another type of material such as potting soil, aquarium gravel, or crumbled modeling clay.

Water Conservation at Home

We all need water. In our homes, we use water to brush our teeth, cook food, and wash clothes. We also use water in countless other ways. Of all the freshwater available on Earth, households use about 8 percent. With available freshwater resources decreasing, it is very important for everyone to conserve water every day.

In this lab activity you will keep a water usage log. You will use your log to suggest ways to conserve water.

Materials   pencil or pen
                   water use log

                   calculator

Procedure

1. Use the table on page 2 to create a water log.

2. For two days, keep track of your family's water usage. Record the usage on your water log.

3. After two days, calculate the amount of water used by your family for each task. Enter this amount in the last column.

4. Calculate the total amount of water used for the week. Record this amount in your notebook.

5. Look over your water log. Suggest ways you and your family could conserve water.

Water Conservation at Home, continued

Water use activity	Number of times used on Day 1	Number of times used on Day 2	Total number of times on both days	Liters used each time	Total liters used on both days
Flush toilet				22.7	
Fill bathtub (5 inches)				151.4	
Shower (5 minutes)				132.5	
Run dishwasher				56.8	
Hand-wash dishes (w/water running)				113.6	
Hand-wash dishes (no water running)				56.8	
Wash car				1,000	
Wash clothes				151.4	
Brush teeth (w/water running)				18.9	
Brush teeth (w/no water on)				1.9	
Wash hands				3.8	
Drink water				0.95	
Water lawn (20 minutes)				567.81	
Totals					

Water Conservation at Home, continued

Analysis

1. Which activity on your water use log used the most water? _____

The least? _____

2. Which activity did your family do most often?

_____

3. Which activity would you consider to be the most wasteful? _____

The least? _____ Explain your answers.

_____

_____

Conclusions

1. Select the five activities that used the most water. Make a list of ways
you and your family could conserve water in these activities.

_____

_____

_____

_____

_____

2. How would your water usage be different if your family had done all of the tasks?

_____

_____

_____

Explore Further

Put your list of ways to save water into use for a week. Redo your
water use log. Were your suggestions successful?

_____

_____

Express Lab 9

Use with Express Lab 9, page 331

Materials air freshener or perfume spray

Procedure

1. Remain seated as your teacher sprays the air freshener or perfume.

2. Raise your hand as soon as you can smell the spray.

3. Compare the smell each person experienced.

Analysis

1. How far away was the spray smelled?

_____

_____

2. How does the spray move through the air?

_____

_____

What Is in the Air?

Use with Investigation 9, pages 333–334

Although you usually cannot feel or see air, it is a substance. Air has mass. Air is filled with many different particles, most of which you do not notice. How can you tell what particles are in the air? Is there a way to capture them and find out? This lab will show you one way to do exactly that.

Materials
cardboard	petroleum jelly
scissors	paper towel
aluminum foil	magnifying glass or
masking tape	microscope
string	

Procedure

1. Cut a 4 cm x 4 cm square from the cardboard.

2. Completely cover the cardboard square with aluminum foil. Make sure that the foil is flat and smooth.

3. Use tape to attach one end of a piece of string to your square.

4. Using a paper towel, cover both sides of the square with a thin, even layer of petroleum jelly. Wipe your hands immediately after using the petroleum jelly. **Safety Alert: Keep the petroleum jelly away from your eyes, nose, and mouth.**

5. Use the string to hang your square in an indoor or outdoor location. Record the specific location. Make notes about the surroundings. For example, is it near a lot of traffic or other source of pollution?

6. Collect your square after 24 hours and examine it with a magnifying glass or microscope.

Cleanup/Disposal

Return the materials and make sure your area is clean before you leave the lab. Wash your hands thoroughly.

What Is in the Air?, continued

Analysis

1. What did you find on your square? Make a list of the things you observed.

   _____

   _____

2. Where do you think these particles come from? Add these notes to your list.

   _____

   _____

Conclusions

1. Compare the types of things found on the squares that were hung outside with the squares that were hung inside. How were they different?

   _____

   _____

2. What do you think you would find in the air of the house of someone who smokes?

   _____

   _____

3. How do air particles affect you?

   _____

   _____

Explore Further

Work with a partner to prepare a presentation of the investigation results. Gather data from all indoor and outdoor squares. Create a visual presentation of the combined results.

_____

_____

_____

_____

How Loud Is Loud?

Sound is all around us. It is part of everyday life. However, some sounds can be considered a form of pollution. Loud, annoying, or constant sounds can cause noise pollution. Sound is measured in units called decibels. On the decibel scale, every 10-point increase is equal to a sound that is 10 times louder. Sounds that are above 85 decibels can cause ear damage or hearing loss. Many of these sounds are classified as noise pollution.

In this lab, you will measure the levels of noise in your school.

Materials   decibel meter
                    pencil or pen
                    ruler
                    graph paper (optional)

Procedure

1. Make a copy of Data Table 1 below on a piece of paper.

Data Table 1

Area of school	Decibel measurement
Classroom	
Hall during class change	
Class change bell/buzzer	
Intercom	
Cafeteria during lunch	
Media center	
Main office	
Gym during PE	
School bus engine	

How Loud Is Loud?, continued

2. Using the decibel meter, take sound readings in the areas of the school listed on Data Table 1.

3. Write down the sound readings in the second column of Data Table 1.

4. Think of two more places in or around your school where you could take sound readings. Write these places in the first column of Data Table 1.

5. Use the decibel meter to take measurements in those areas. Record the measurements in the second column of Data Table 1.

6. Compare your measurements to the ones on Data Table 2.

Data Table 2

Common sounds	Decibel level	Effects or descriptions of sounds
Rocket launch	180	irreversible hearing loss
Siren	140	painfully loud
Jet takeoff	130	painful
Rock concert	120	extremely loud (hearing loss after 15 min)
Thunderclap	110	extremely loud
Garbage truck	100	very loud
Lawn mower	90	very annoying
Alarm clock	80	annoying (hearing loss after 8 hours)
Noisy restaurant	70	very intrusive
Normal conversation	60	intrusive
Light auto traffic	50	quiet
Refrigerator hum	40	quiet
Library	30	very quiet
Soft whisper	20	very quiet

How Loud Is Loud?, continued

Cleanup/Disposal

Dispose of the materials according to your teacher's instructions.

Analysis

1. Of the sounds you recorded, which was the loudest?

   _____

2. Of the sounds you recorded, which was the quietest?

   _____

3. Of the sounds you recorded, which could cause hearing loss?

   _____

   _____

Conclusions

1. List the sounds you recorded in order from the softest to the loudest.

   _____

2. To what common sounds in Data Table 2 did your softest sounds compare? Your loudest?

   _____

   _____

3. In the areas where you recorded sounds that were 60 decibels or higher, suggest ways to decrease noise levels.

   _____

   _____

Explore Further

Using the decibel meter, take sound readings in several parts of your community. Evaluate the data you collect to decide which areas are suffering from noise pollution.

   _____

   _____

Colors and Heat

Use with Discovery Investigation 9, pages 340–341

The colors of building materials can contribute to the urban heat island effect. How much does color affect the amount of heat that is absorbed? Which colors absorb more heat? You will find out in this lab.

Materials   colored ceramic tiles or paint chips   stopwatch, or clock with
          2 clear drinking glasses or plastic cups   a second hand
          2 thermometers   heat lamp or strong sunlight

Procedure

1. In a small group, select two colors of the same material, such as ceramic tiles or paint chips. Choose a very dark color and a very light color.

2. Write a hypothesis about the amount of heat each item will absorb.

3. Write a procedure and Safety Alerts for your experiment, using the materials listed.

4. Have your hypothesis, Safety Alerts, and procedure approved by your teacher. Then perform your experiment.

5. Collect and record data. Use your data to create a graph that shows the temperatures of the different-colored materials at different time intervals.

Cleanup/Disposal

Return the materials and make sure your area is clean before you leave the lab.

Analysis

1. Was your hypothesis correct? Explain why or why not.

   _____

   _____

2. What color absorbed the most heat? Explain.

   _____

   _____

Colors and Heat, continued

3. What color absorbed the least heat? Explain.

_____

_____

Conclusions

1. What color would be good to use on a house in a cold climate? Explain your answer.

_____

_____

2. What color would be good to use on a house in a hot climate? Explain your answer.

_____

_____

3. Contrast how light- and dark-colored materials interact with energy from the lamp or the sun.

_____

_____

Explore Further

Take the paint chip that, according to your data, absorbed the most heat. Cut pieces of another color and glue these pieces to the paint chip. How do you think this will affect the original paint chip's ability to absorb heat? Write a hypothesis and test it.

_____

_____

_____

_____

The Case of the Disappearing Statues

Marble buildings and statues are disappearing. Marble is made out of calcium carbonate. Two other familiar forms of calcium carbonate are chalk and limestone. Acid rain dissolves all of these. Over time, acid rain slowly wears away the surfaces of marble buildings and statues.

In this lab activity, you will observe the effect of acid on calcium carbonate.

Materials

safety goggles	100-mL graduated cylinder
lab coat or apron	250-mL beaker
pieces of white chalk	digital scale
vinegar	forceps
water	

Procedure

1. Put on safety goggles and a lab coat or apron.

2. Copy the following data table on a piece of paper.

Weight of chalk before acid	
Weight of chalk after acid	
Amount of chalk dissolved	

3. Measure 50 mL of vinegar in the graduated cylinder.

4. Pour the vinegar into the beaker.

5. Add 150 mL of water to the beaker.

6. Get a piece of white chalk and weigh it on the digital scale. Record the weight on the data table.

7. Break the chalk in half and place both halves into the beaker. Observe any changes you see.

8. After one hour, use forceps to remove the chalk pieces. Allow them to dry.

9. Weigh the dry pieces on the digital scale. Record the weight on your data table.

The Case of the Disappearing Statues, continued

Cleanup/Disposal

Dispose of the materials according to your teacher's instructions.

Analysis

1. What happened in the beaker when you added the chalk?

   _____

   _____

2. How much chalk was dissolved by the acid in the beaker?

   _____

Conclusions

1. In this experiment, what do the vinegar and water represent?

   _____

2. What does the chalk represent? _____

3. What do you think would happen to the chalk if it were left in the
   beaker for several weeks? _____

   _____

4. If statues and buildings are exposed to acid rain for a long time,
   what will happen to them? _____

   _____

   _____

Explore Further

Find pictures of buildings and statues that have been affected by acid
rain. Examine the pictures closely with a magnifying glass. Estimate the
percentage of each structure that has been lost due to acid rain.

_____

_____

_____

_____

Express Lab 10

Use with Express Lab 10, page 363

Materials   latex gloves
2 clean, wide-mouthed glass jars
2 plastic bags
masking tape
2 pieces of garbage

Procedure

1. Put on the latex gloves.

2. Select a piece of garbage you think is biodegradable.

3. Select a piece you think is not biodegradable.

4. Place one piece of garbage in each jar.

5. Place a plastic bag over each jar, and seal the bag with tape.

6. Observe both jars over the next two days.

Analysis

1. Describe any differences in how each bag looks.

   _____

   _____

2. Which material do you think is biodegradable? How can you tell?

   _____

   _____

De-inking Paper

Use with Investigation 10, pages 371–372

Before printed paper can be made into recycled paper, it must pass through several steps. First, the paper must be ground into a pulp. Then the ink must be removed. This process is called de-inking. Several steps are needed to de-ink paper. In this lab, you will turn printed paper into pulp and begin to de-ink it.

Materials	safety goggles	eyedropper
	lab coat or apron	dish detergent
	several sheets of printed copier paper	plastic tray
		spoon
	plastic bowl	drinking straws
	hand-operated mixer	several sheets of filter paper
	hot tap water	magnifying glass

Procedure

1. In a group, make a data table like the one shown below.

Sample	Description
1	
2	
3	
4	

2. Put on safety goggles and a lab coat or apron.

3. Tear printed copier paper into 4-cm squares. Place the squares in a bowl.

4. Add 1 liter of hot tap water to the bowl. Place the bowl on a plastic tray. Then use the eyedropper to add 5–10 drops of detergent to the bowl. Use the hand-operated mixer to mix for three minutes.

5. Scoop out half a spoonful of the paper mixture, called pulp, onto a piece of filter paper. Label this Sample 1 and set it aside to dry.

De-inking Paper, continued

6. Have each group member hold a separate straw in the mixture and blow through the straw. Continue blowing for 5 minutes, taking breaths every 15 seconds or as often as necessary. **Safety Alert: Be careful not to suck up the paper mixture through the straw. If you feel dizzy, stop blowing and breathe normally. Keep track of which straw is yours. Do not share straws.**

7. As you blow, bubbles will form. Use the spoon to scoop the bubbles onto the tray.

8. Repeat Step 5 and label it Sample 2. Make sure you scoop out the pulp, not the foamy bubbles.

9. Examine both samples of pulp with a magnifying glass. Record your observations.

10. Repeat Steps 6–9 two more times.

Cleanup/Disposal

Before you leave the lab, clean your work area and wash your hands.

Analysis

1. Summarize the appearance of each sample of paper pulp.

_____

_____

2. During what part of the investigation is the ink removed?

_____

Conclusions

1. Which sample of pulp would be best for making recycled copier paper?

_____

2. What other steps may be needed to make sure all the ink color is gone?

_____

_____

Explore Further

Repeat the experiment using different types of paper or detergent.

Hazardous Materials Survey

Your home probably contains material that could be classified as hazardous waste. Cleaning products often include chemicals that can harm the environment. By reading the labels on these products, we can dispose of them correctly. Proper disposal of hazardous products keeps them from polluting the environment.

In this lab, you will identify hazardous materials in your home.

Materials   hazardous material chart
                     pencil or pen
                     household cleaning materials

Procedure

1. Make a copy of the data table below.

Area of the house	Cleaning products	Main chemical	Manufacturer's warnings or suggestions for disposal
Kitchen			
Bathroom			
Laundry			

2. Identify two cleaning products that can be used to clean the kitchen. List them in the second column of the data table.

3. Identify the main cleaning chemical in each product. Usually, it will be listed first and may be in large, dark print.

Hazardous Materials Survey, continued

4. For each product, read the label for recommendations for disposal. Are there any warnings about harming the environment or living things included on the label? If so, list them.

5. Repeat the same procedure for products used to clean the bathroom and laundry.

Cleanup/Disposal

Dispose of the materials according to your teacher's instructions.

Analysis

1. Which products are the most hazardous? _____

_____

2. Which products have warnings about the environment? _____

_____

3. What were some warnings the products have concerning living things?

_____

_____

Conclusions

1. Of kitchen, laundry, and bathroom cleaners, which products are the most hazardous?

_____

2. What was the most common method of disposal for these products?

_____

_____

3. Why do you think it is important to read labels on products like these before you use them?

_____

_____

Explore Further

Find out what kinds of cleaning products are safe for the environment. Try using them at home.

Mineral Recycling

Minerals like copper and iron are mined to make products that everyone uses. Some of these products include steel, cooking pans, and electrical wire. Each day, land is destroyed by strip mining to remove these minerals from the earth. Many mining companies repair the land after strip mining. However, the land can never be put back exactly the way it was. That is why it is very important to recycle minerals that have already been mined.

In this lab activity, you will model mineral recycling by copper plating an iron nail.

Materials

safety goggles	string
lab coat or apron	craft stick
10–15 dull pennies (pre-1982 work best)	250-mL beaker
	teaspoon
ungalvanized iron nail	magnifying glass
vinegar	paper towel
salt	

Procedure

1. Put on safety goggles and a lab coat or apron.

2. Pour 100 mL of vinegar into the beaker and stir in a teaspoon of salt.

3. Add the dull pennies to the vinegar-and-salt solution.

4. Gently swirl the beaker for 10 minutes. Observe what happens to the surface of the pennies. Record your observations on a piece of paper.

5. Remove the pennies from the beaker with the teaspoon. Set the pennies aside. Do not pour out the liquid.

6. Tie a piece of string to the nail. Tie the other end of the string to the center of a craft stick.

7. Place the nail in the beaker. Rotate the craft stick to wind up string so that the nail is suspended under the liquid.

8. Observe the nail for 30 minutes. Use a magnifying glass to inspect it closely.

9. Remove the nail and lay it on a paper towel to dry.

Mineral Recycling, continued

Cleanup/Disposal

Dispose of the materials according to your teacher's instructions.

Analysis

1. How did the pennies look before you placed them in the beaker?

   _____

2. How did the pennies look after you removed them from the beaker?

   _____

3. What formed on the nail while it was in the liquid?

   _____

4. What color did the nail turn?

   _____

Conclusions

1. The vinegar and salt formed a mild acid. How did this acid affect the pennies?

   _____

2. What material do you think coated the nail? _____

   Where do you think the material came from? _____

   _____

3. In this lab, you plated an iron nail with copper from pennies. Your experiment
   mimics the process of copper recycling. List some other ways you think
   that minerals could be recycled. _____

   _____

4. Some cooking pans have copper bottoms. Based on the experiment, how
   do you think the copper was put on the cooking pans?

   _____

   _____

Explore Further

Use the Internet to research some other ways to recycle minerals.

Landfill Design
Use with Discovery Investigation 10, pages 385–386

Modern sanitary landfills are designed to hold garbage safely. A landfill site is designed to help prevent water pollution. Still, some liquids leak from landfills. How? Explore some possible answers by designing and building a model landfill.

Materials

safety goggles	plastic grocery bag
lab coat or apron	soil
two 2-liter plastic bottles	yellow sponge
scissors	water
gravel	red or green food coloring
blue sponge	plastic cup

Procedure

1. Cut the top one-third off of a plastic bottle. Cut the bottom one-third off of the other plastic bottle. **Safety Alert: Be extremely careful when cutting the plastic bottles with scissors.** You should be able to assemble the pieces as shown on page 385 of the textbook.

2. Cut the sponges to make circular disks that will fit snugly in a soda bottle. The yellow sponge stands for garbage and the blue sponge stands for groundwater. From the grocery bag, cut a circle of plastic slightly larger than the bottle's diameter. This stands for a plastic liner in a landfill.

3. Gather the remainder of the materials. Use the diagram of a plastic bottle landfill on page 385 as a guide for making your own model. You can vary the placement and amount of materials. You do not have to use all of the materials.

4. In your lab group, discuss the features of a landfill and their purposes. Speculate about how a landfill could pollute groundwater, as well as ways this could be prevented. Write a hypothesis about how well landfills prevent leachate from escaping that could be tested with an experiment that uses the materials shown.

5. Write a procedure for your experiment. Include Safety Alerts.

6. Have your hypothesis, procedure, and Safety Alerts approved by your teacher. Then carry out your experiment. Record your results.

Landfill Design, continued

Cleanup/Disposal

Put away all materials and clean your work area before leaving the lab.

Analysis

1. What were the important differences between your group's landfill models and those of other groups?

   _____

   _____

2. Compare the leaked liquid that came from each model.

   _____

   _____

Conclusions

1. Which features of a sanitary landfill help prevent pollution?

   _____

   _____

2. Why must the leachate from landfills be monitored for many years?

   _____

   _____

Explore Further

Repeat the experiment using coffee grounds to represent garbage instead of a yellow sponge.

_____

_____

_____

_____

The Living Soil

Soil is an abiotic part of the environment. However, soil contains living things. Bacteria, fungi, and microorganisms are soil inhabitants. These living things help make soil fertile. Organisms that live in soil break down the remains of plants and animals and recycle their nutrients.

In this lab, you will observe the living components of topsoil.

Materials   safety goggles   gauze

                      lab coat or apron   magnifying glass

                      soil samples   lamp

                      funnel   access to the library

                      glass jar   or Internet

Procedure

1. Collect a sample of soil and bring it to class before the lab activity. Collect soil from an area where there is some dead or decaying plant material on the soil.

2. Put on safety goggles and a lab coat or apron.

3. Place the funnel in the glass jar.

4. Line the funnel with gauze.

5. Put the soil sample on top of the gauze.

6. Position the jar and funnel under a lamp overnight. The soil organisms will move away from the lamp. They will travel toward the bottom of the funnel. Some organisms will drop through the bottom of the funnel and fall into the jar.

7. The next day, use the magnifying glass to observe the organisms that collect in the jar.

Cleanup/Disposal

Dispose of the materials according to your teacher's instructions.

The Living Soil, continued

Analysis

1. On a piece of paper, draw some of the organisms you observed.

_____

_____

2. Identify some of these organisms. Use books from the library or the Internet to find their names.

_____

_____

Conclusions

1. Why do you think the organisms moved away from the light?

_____

_____

2. What are some organisms that may be in your soil sample that you could not see? _____

_____

3. Why was it important to collect soil whose surface was covered with dead plant and animal matter?

_____

_____

Explore Further

Observe a small sample of soil under a microscope to see some of the microorganisms present. Draw what you observe. Then identify some of the organisms.

_____

_____

_____

_____

Express Lab 11

Use with Express Lab 11, page 403

Materials   tray
soil
pencil
watering can

Procedure

1. Create two mounds of soil in the tray. Make sure the mounds are as similar as possible, with the same height and the same slope.

2. Use the pencil to "plow" rows on each pile. On the first mound, make rows that are parallel to the slope, following the contours of the mound. On the second mound, make rows that are perpendicular to the slope.

3. Sprinkle both slopes with the same amount of water from the watering can. Observe the soil that collects at the bottom of each mound.

Analysis

1. Which mound eroded the most?

_____

_____

2. How does contour farming help reduce erosion?

_____

_____

How Are Soils Different?

Use with Investigation 11, pages 404–405

You probably do not think about the soil under your feet very often. However, soil is a very important resource. We grow our food in it and plant trees and flowers in it. Are soils really that different from place to place? What different properties do they have? In this lab, you will find out.

Materials   safety goggles   variety of soil sifters

lab coat or apron   magnifying glass

sandy soil   paper towels

clay soil   plastic tray

potting soil

Procedure

1. Put on safety goggles and a lab coat or apron. **Safety Alert: Do not rub your eyes if your fingers are dirty.**

2. Get a cup of the sandy soil.

3. Pass the soil through the coarsest sifter (the one with the largest holes). Be sure to put a paper towel underneath to catch the soil that passes through.

4. Place what the sifter keeps in a pile on the tray.

5. Use the soil that passed through the sifter and pass it through the next finer sifter. Again, place what the sifter keeps in a pile on the tray.

6. Repeat Step 5 using the next finest sifter. You should have several piles of soil sorted by particle size.

7. Examine the particles in each pile. Record your observations.

8. Repeat Steps 3–7 for the clay soil and the potting soil. Make notes on what you observe in each sample, as well as the amount of soil that sifts out at different sizes.

Cleanup/Disposal

Dispose of your soil samples according to your teacher's instructions. Make sure your work surface is clean.

How Are Soils Different?, continued

Analysis

1. How did the particle size of the potting soil compare to the particle sizes of the sandy soil and the clay soil?

_____

_____

2. What other differences did you observe between the soils?

_____

_____

Conclusions

1. What relationship did you find between the size and type of soil particles and how well plants grow in the soil?

_____

_____

2. How easy would it be for water to move through the different types of soil? How might that affect what plants can grow in each type of soil?

_____

_____

Explore Further

Collect a soil sample from your yard or outside your school. Run your sample through the soil sifters and examine it with the magnifying glass. Which type of soil does it most closely resemble?

_____

_____

_____

Using Food Labels for Better Nutrition

Use with Discovery Investigation 11, pages 411–412

How do you know exactly what you are eating? Read the labels. Almost every food product you buy has a nutrition label on the package that tells you what it contains. How can you use food labels to monitor your diet and maintain good health? You can design a lab to find out.

Materials paper and pencil
variety of food labels

Procedure

1. Examine several food labels. In your lab group, discuss the different parts of the labels. Include the list of ingredients, the nutrition information, and the calories per serving.

2. Write a hypothesis about how you can use food labels and other nutrition information to improve your nutrition.

3. Write a procedure to test your hypothesis. You may want to carry out your procedure over a week as you track the nutrition of your diet. Have your hypothesis, procedure, and any Safety Alerts approved by your teacher.

4. Carry out your procedure. Record your results.

Cleanup/Disposal

Return any packaged food and labels as directed by your teacher.

Analysis

1. How many calories did you consume during the day? How many are recommended?

   _____

   _____

   _____

2. Make a data table or graph that shows how much protein, carbohydrates, fat, and fiber are recommended and how much you consumed.

Using Food Labels for Better Nutrition, continued

3. What is likely to happen to someone who regularly eats more calories than is recommended? What is likely to happen to someone who regularly eats fewer calories than is recommended?

_____

_____

_____

Conclusions

1. How did your diet compare to the recommended daily allowances?

_____

_____

2. What nutrients did you not get enough of in your daily diet?

_____

_____

3. In what ways could you improve your diet?

_____

_____

Explore Further

Write a description of three fast-food meals. Use the Internet or other research to obtain nutrition information about these foods. How would a daily diet of fast food compare to the daily recommended allowances?

_____

_____

_____

_____

Produce Production

The produce department of a grocery store contains fresh fruits and vegetables. When you are grocery shopping, you may not think about where the produce comes from. Every day, grocery stores sell produce from local farmers, other states, and other countries. Grocery stores keep fruits and vegetables all year, regardless of growing season. Some produce items cost more than others to purchase. The growing season, distance traveled, and time in storage are three things that determine the cost of produce.

In this lab, you will survey a local grocery store produce department.

Materials   access to a grocery store
paper
pen or pencil

Procedure

   1. Make a copy of the table below.

Fruits			Vegetables		
Item	Origin	Cost	Item	Origin	Cost

   2. Make a trip to the produce department at a local grocery store.

   3. Look for fruits and vegetables that have bags or stickers that identify their place of origin. If some are not marked, you can ask the produce manager about their origin.

   4. Select five fruits and five vegetables.

   5. Write their names in the column labeled *Item*. For each, write down their place of origin in the column labeled *Origin*.

Produce Production, continued

6. Write down the cost of each in the column labeled *Cost.*

7. If possible, take the stickers or containers of the fruits and vegetables to class.

Analysis

1. What is the origin of most of the produce you inspected: local, other states, or other countries? _____

2. Which of the items you selected was the most expensive? _____

Suggest a reason why it was the most expensive. _____

_____

_____

Conclusions

1. Total the number of items grown locally, imported from other states, or imported from other countries. Write the totals on the table below.

2. Obtain a class total for each category to complete the table.

	Grown locally	Imported from other states	Imported from other countries
Your total			
Class total			

3. How did the distance the produce traveled affect the price of the produce?

_____

_____

Explore Further

Select one of your items and research the path it took from the farm to the grocery store.

Express Lab 12

Use with Express Lab 12, page 435

Materials   sample of pond water
eyedropper
microscope slide
cover slip
microscope

Procedure

1. Use an eyedropper to get a small amount of a pond water sample.

2. Place one drop of the pond water in the center of a microscope slide.

3. Cover the drop with a cover slip.

4. Observe the pond water under low power of a microscope.

5. Switch to high power to get a closer view of any living things you find.

Analysis

1. How many different kinds of organisms did you observe?

_____

_____

_____

2. Would you rate the biodiversity of the pond water as low, medium, or high? Explain your answer.

_____

_____

_____

Using an Identification Key

Use with Investigation 12, pages 443–444

Have you noticed the many different kinds of flowering plants that grow along a roadside? Do you know what species they are? It is easy to find out if you know how to use an identification key. A key has sets of contrasting descriptions. A number or letter for another set follows each description. Sometimes, a species name follows a description. In this lab, you will use a key to identify the species a plant belongs to.

Materials   gloves
              roadside plants
              native plant key
              hand lens
              razor blade

Procedure

1. Put on gloves.

2. Select a plant to identify.

3. Get an identification key from your teacher.

4. Observe the plant for general characteristics. Use the glossary of the key to find out what any unfamiliar terms mean.

5. Start with the first set (usually a pair) of descriptions.

6. Decide which description fits the plant. Record the number and/or letter at the end of that description.

7. Find the set of descriptions with the number/letter you wrote down.

8. Repeat Steps 5 and 6 several times, if needed. When a scientific name follows a description you choose, you have identified the plant.

9. Read the description of that plant species to be sure you found the correct name. If the description does not fit, repeat Steps 4–7.

Cleanup/Disposal

Before you leave the lab, be sure your work area is clean. Return your identification key and plant sample to your teacher.

Using an Identification Key, continued

Analysis

1. Did you find the correct species name for your plant on the first try? Explain.

   _____

   _____

2. What should you do if the first name you find is incorrect?

   _____

   _____

3. Which of the words in the identification key did you find most difficult to understand?

   _____

   _____

Conclusions

1. What is the scientific name of the plant you identified?

   _____

   _____

2. Why must you work through the sets of descriptions in the order indicated?

   _____

   _____

Explore Further

Choose another plant and repeat the steps in the lab.

Schoolyard Biodiversity

Biodiversity is the number of different species of organisms in an environment. Generally, an area with a lot of biodiversity is more stable than one with only a little biodiversity. Worldwide, biodiversity is decreasing. One of the major reasons is loss of habitat. As habitat is lost, more and more species become endangered. Ultimately, these species may become extinct.

In this lab activity, you will survey biodiversity in your area by making a leaf collection.

Materials

six 8 cm x 10 cm pieces of corrugated cardboard	scissors
several pieces of newsprint that are cut to fit the cardboard	four #64 rubber bands
	index cards
waxed paper	tree and leaf identification books
tape	science notebook
	heavy books (optional)

Procedure, Leaf Collection

1. Following your teacher's instructions, collect five leaves from different trees or shrubs.

2. As you collect each leaf, write the date and location in your science notebook.

Procedure, Construction of Leaf Press

1. Place two pieces of newsprint on top of a piece of cardboard.

2. Lay one leaf in the center of the newsprint.

3. Place two more pieces of newsprint on top of the leaf.

4. Add another piece of cardboard, two pieces of newsprint, a leaf, then two pieces of newsprint.

5. Continue Steps 1–4 until you have placed all of your leaves in the leaf press.

6. Wrap a rubber band around each end of the leaf press and on the sides to hold the cardboard in place.

Schoolyard Biodiversity, continued

Procedure, Leaf Preservation

1. Place the leaf press under two or three heavy books.

2. After three days, remove the leaves from the press.

3. Cut a piece of waxed paper large enough to fold around one leaf.

4. Seal the edges of the waxed paper with tape.

5. Repeat Steps 3 and 4 for each leaf.

Procedure, Leaf Identification

1. Obtain an index card for each leaf.

2. Use a tree identification book or other resource to identify each of your leaves.

3. On each card, write the common and scientific names, date collected, and location collected.

4. Attach the card to the waxed paper with the leaf.

Analysis

1. How many different types of leaves did you collect?

   _____

   _____

2. How many different types of leaves was your class able to find?

   _____

   _____

Schoolyard Biodiversity, continued

Conclusions

1. Do you consider the biodiversity of trees and shrubs in your
   area to be low or high? Why?

   _____

   _____

2. Suggest ways that you could increase biodiversity in your area.

   _____

   _____

3. List some other organisms that would benefit from living in an area
   with a high tree biodiversity.

   _____

   _____

Explore Further

Carry out research to find out if the trees and shrubs in your area
are native species.

_____

_____

_____

_____

Exploring Local Species Richness
Use with Discovery Investigation 12, pages 451–452

How many different species of plants live on your school grounds? Species richness is one measure of biodiversity. You can estimate local species richness by identifying the number of different species in an area. This means identifying the species of each living thing you observe. How can you best do that? In this lab, you will explore the species richness of plants in your local area. You will use keys and field guides to help you identify species.

Materials   disposable gloves

field notebook

magnifying glass

field guides and keys

Procedure

1. In your lab group, discuss the idea of species richness and how it can be measured.

2. Choose a specific area of your school grounds to investigate.

3. Decide how you will sample and record these different plant species in the area you have chosen.

4. Create a hypothesis about the amount of diversity in your area. Then write a procedure for your investigation. Include Safety Alerts.

5. Have your hypothesis, procedure, and Safety Alerts approved by your teacher. Then carry out your investigation. Record your results.

Cleanup/Disposal

Be sure to collect all your materials before returning to the lab.

Exploring Local Species Richness, continued

Analysis

1. Summarize the results of your investigation.

   _____

   _____

2. How did your estimate of species richness compare with estimates made by other groups?

   _____

   _____

Conclusions

1. Was your hypothesis supported by the results of your experiment?

   _____

   _____

2. Do you think the animal species richness is similar to that of the plants in the area? Explain.

   _____

   _____

3. Suppose you continue your investigation and expand it to a wider area. How is your estimate of the area's species richness likely to change?

   _____

   _____

Explore Further

Estimate the species richness in other locations, such as your backyard or a local park.

   _____

   _____

   _____

   _____

Making Decisions About the Environment

You make several decisions every day. Most are simple, such as what to wear to school or which movie to watch. Other types of decisions are complex. Deciding what to do about an environmental issue can be difficult. Often, values are important factors in making environmental decisions. As you read in Chapter 1, values are the beliefs that determine people's actions.

In this lab, you will use the values you find important to make a decision regarding the environment.

Materials
    pencil
    ruler or meter stick
    paper
    markers (optional)
    poster board (optional)

Procedure

1. On a piece of paper, draw a data table like the one below.

Consequences	Values			
Positive short-term consequences				
Negative short-term consequences				
Positive long-term consequences				
Negative long-term consequences				

Making Decisions About the Environment, continued

2. Read, the text below about the environmental issue facing the community of Terminus:

For years, the Terminus highway system has efficiently moved people to and from work. Recently, the land near the northern suburbs has been under development. New businesses and subdivisions are being built there. This development is putting a strain on the highway system. The roads have become overcrowded, slowing travel. People are spending more and more time traveling to work. The number of traffic accidents has increased. Also, the local weather bureau has noticed an increase in air pollution.

To solve these problems, the city council proposes the construction of a rapid-transit system. Their proposal includes electric trains that will connect the northern suburbs to the downtown. The trains, they say, will provide clean, fast, and reliable transportation. The proposed train tracks will pass through a wilderness area and a local park. The city council hopes that the trains will be more important to the community than the loss of the wilderness and the park. In order to fund the trains, the city council will have to raise taxes. However, the council points out that the system will pay for itself in a few years due to the riders' fees.

3. Review the following list of values: aesthetic, recreational, scientific, social/cultural, health, ethical/moral, educational, environmental, and economic. Think about which ones apply most to the situation facing the people of Terminus.

4. Select four values that you think the community should consider in making their decision. Write those values at the top of columns 2 through 5 on the data table.

5. For each value you listed, think carefully about the short-term and long-term consequences of the decision. Consequences can be positive and negative.

6. Complete your data table by writing the consequences of each value.

7. Based upon your completed data table, decide what you think the people of Terminus should do. Write your decision on your paper.

8. Make a poster of your completed data table and your solution. Present this information to the class.

Making Decisions About the Environment, continued

Analysis

1. What is the decision that the people of Terminus must make?

_____

_____

2. In your evaluation, did you think short-term or long-term consequences were the most important? Why?

_____

_____

Conclusions

1. How did the values selected by other classmates compare to yours?

_____

_____

2. How did the decision you reached compare with decisions made by the rest of the class?

_____

_____

Explore Further

Research an environmental decision that faces your community. Use this method to offer a possible solution.

_____

_____

_____

_____

Competition in the Grassland

Grasslands are very large biomes with few shrubs or trees. They receive more rain than deserts but not enough to support large plants. Grasslands are very important to people. They are the places where we grow most of our food crops, such as wheat and corn. As farming increases, less land is left for native grasses. As a result, many native grasses are disappearing. This can affect the entire ecosystem in a negative way.

In this lab activity, you will grow different grasses to determine which is the most successful.

Materials

safety goggles

lab coat or apron

3 small flowerpots

3 aluminum pie pans

potting soil

native grass seeds (buffalo grass is recommended)

nonnative grass seeds (fescue or rye are recommended)

water

metric ruler

magnifying glass

grow light (optional)

graph paper

science notebook

Procedure

1. Put on safety goggles and a lab coat or apron.

2. Place equal amounts of potting soil into each of the three pots. Fill them almost to the top.

3. Label the pots as *A*, *B*, and *C*.

4. Add the grass seeds to the pots as follows:

   Pot A: native grass seeds only

   Pot B: nonnative seeds only

   Pot C: equal amounts of both seeds

5. Loosely cover the seeds with a layer of potting soil.

6. Place each pot onto a pie plate and water the soil until moist. Make sure to add the same amount of water to each pot.

Competition in the Grassland, continued

7. Place the pots in a well-lit area or under a grow light.

8. Observe the pots on a daily basis. If the soil becomes dry, add equal amounts of water to each pot.

9. Make three data tables like the one below in your science notebook.

Pot _____	Seed Type(s) _____	
	Maximum height	Number of leaves
Day 1		
Day 2		
Day 3		
Day 4		
Day 5		
Day 6		
Day 7		

10. As the grasses begin to grow, measure the height of the tallest plant in each pot in millimeters. Record the height on the data table.

11. Count the number of leaves on the tallest plant in each pot. Record the number of leaves on the data table.

12. Continue to measure the plants and count leaves for seven days.

Competition in the Grassland, continued

Analysis

1. In this lab, which pot(s) is/are the experimental group(s)?

_____

2. Which pot(s) is/are the control(s)?

_____

3. What other things do you have to control in this experiment?

_____

Conclusions

1. In which pot did the grass grow the tallest? In which pot was the grass the shortest?

_____

2. How did the growth of the grasses in Pots A and B compare with the growth in Pot C?

_____

_____

_____

3. In which pot was there competition?

_____

4. For what resources did the grasses have to compete?

_____

5. In Pot C, which of the two grasses seemed to grow taller?

_____

Explore Further

How would grazing animals affect the growth of the grasses? Simulate this by clipping the grasses in each pot. Observe the growth of the clipped grass over a period of two weeks.

_____

_____

Express Lab 13

Use with Express Lab 13, page 480

Materials   map or photo of a local park or wildlife preserve

Procedure

1. Discuss the different things that the park or preserve provides to the community.

2. Create a data table. Include the name of each resource and its estimated value. If you cannot describe the value in dollars, write a description of what the resource provides.

Analysis

1. What types of things could you not estimate a value for in dollars?

   _____

   _____

2. How else could you measure the value of these things?

   _____

   _____

Creating Sustainable Communities

Use with Investigation 13, pages 487–488

Sustainable communities must find the resources they need while maintaining the health of the environment. They must also deal with issues such as transportation, community planning, pollution, and economic health. In this lab, you will work to plan a sustainable community.

Materials   Internet and library reference materials
materials to create a poster or presentation

Procedure

1. Form a small group to discuss what characteristics are necessary in a sustainable community. Have someone be the recorder and write down the characteristics of this imaginary community.

2. Determine the size of your community. The population can vary. It may have 20 or 30 people. It may also be a large city with a million people.

3. Determine where your community exists, what surrounds it, and what natural resources are available.

4. You might also consider some of the following aspects when planning your sustainable community:

   • What jobs are needed?

   • How will you get resources?

   • How will you deal with waste and pollution?

   • What are your needs for public transportation, health, etc.?

   • What indicators will you monitor to determine success and failure?

5. Present your plan to the class as a poster or presentation. Include a drawing of your imaginary community.

6. Compare your plans with those of other groups in your class.

Cleanup/Disposal

Return any materials and make sure your area is clean.

Creating Sustainable Communities, continued

Analysis

1. Which ideas did your group have that were unique?

   _____

   _____

2. Which ideas were used by more than one group?

   _____

   _____

3. What decisions did your group face as you created the plan for your sustainable community?

   _____

   _____

Conclusions

1. How are the needs and concerns of a small community different from those of a large community?

   _____

   _____

2. Why is it important to be able to publicly discuss sustainable policies and actions?

   _____

   _____

Explore Further

Research one or more of the sustainable community projects currently going on in the United States. Compare these communities to the one you created.

_____

_____

_____

_____

Being a Green Consumer

To maintain a sustainable environment, everyone must work together. As a consumer, you can do your part by choosing products that reduce pollution. When you select products that are recyclable, biodegradable, or nonpolluting, you are "buying green." Green represents the color of the healthy environment. For "green" products to sell, they must be just as effective as their competitors.

In this lab, you will make a "green" window cleaner. Then you will compare the effectiveness of a popular window spray with your window cleaner.

Materials	safety goggles	water
	lab coat or apron	store-brand window cleaner
	spray bottle	paper towels
	vegetable oil-based liquid soap	masking tape
	white vinegar	access to several glass windows

Procedure

1. Put on safety goggles and a lab coat or apron.

2. Pour 500 mL of water into the spray bottle.

3. Add 3 mL of vegetable oil-based liquid soap and 45 mL of white vinegar.

4. Place the spray nozzle onto the bottle and gently swirl it to mix the ingredients.

5. Divide a dirty window in half with a piece of tape.

6. In your notebook, write a hypothesis as to which cleaner you think will be most effective.

7. Spray one side of the window with your green cleaner. Wipe the window with paper towels.

8. Spray the other side of the window with the store-brand cleaner. Try to spray the same amount. Wipe this side with new paper towels.

9. Observe the windows and compare the results. Record your observations in your science notebook.

Cleanup/Disposal

Dispose of the materials according to your teacher's instructions.

Being a Green Consumer, continued

Analysis

1. How well did your green cleaner get the dirt off the window compared to the store brand?

_____

_____

2. Did your hypothesis agree with the results?

_____

3. Why did you have to spray the same amount of cleaner on each half of the window?

_____

_____

Conclusions

1. Read the label on the store-brand window cleaner. List some of the ingredients that you think might pollute the environment.

_____

2. Would you be willing to use your nonpolluting cleaner instead of the store brand? Why or why not?

_____

_____

3. Suggest other products that you could buy or make that would be considered green.

_____

_____

Explore Further

Find out what other kinds of green cleaners you can make. Compare their effectiveness to store-brand cleaners.

Getting Involved

Use with Discovery Investigation 13, pages 495–496

Protecting the environment and creating sustainable communities requires action from both the government of a country and its citizens. Citizens have a right and responsibility to learn about the policies and issues their community faces. Being informed allows people to vote and participate in important government decisions.

How can you become a better-informed citizen? In this lab, you will research the different citizen action groups and issues in your local area. You will learn and use the skills that will help you become an informed voter.

Materials   Internet and library reference materials

                pencil

                paper

Procedure

1. Work in pairs or small groups to research local environmental issues. You may use the Internet or your local newspaper to find recent news about environmental issues.

2. Create a list of citizen action groups found in your state. Research which of your local issues each group might take an interest in.

3. Choose one issue and obtain materials about it from your state's citizen action groups.

4. Find out the opinions on both sides of the issue. Read editorials from major newspapers or other media concerning your issue.

5. Have your group agree upon a position about the issue. Write a paper explaining your group's position.

6. Use your paper to prepare a letter to the editor of your local newspaper. Sign your letter as a group and send it in.

Cleanup/Disposal

Return the materials and make sure your area is clean.

Getting Involved, continued

Analysis

1. Which issue did your group choose for your research? Explain why.

   _____

   _____

2. What action was recommended by the citizen action group?
   Do you agree or disagree with this opinion?

   _____

   _____

Conclusions

1. How do citizen action groups, newspapers, and other types of participants
   play an important role in determining environmental policies?

   _____

   _____

2. How do you think citizen action groups can be helpful?

   _____

   _____

Explore Further

Find the outcome of an environmental issue that was voted on recently
in your area. Then find out what the voter turnout was for that day. If possible,
calculate the percentage of eligible voters who voted that day.

_____

_____

_____

_____